STRENGTHS
BASED
MARRIAGE

PRAISE FOR *STRENGTHS BASED MARRIAGE*

"What an incredible book for couples! We've been waiting for a resource like this and Jimmy and Allan are just the two to write it. Don't miss out on this grounded, practical, and invaluable message."

—Drs. Les and Leslie Parrott, #1 *New York Times* bestselling
authors of *Saving Your Marriage Before It Starts*

"I can't think of two people more qualified to write a book about how to have a strengths-based marriage than leading marriage expert Jimmy Evans and strengths coach Allan Kelsey. You'll discover how you were uniquely created and how your strengths allow you to connect with your spouse on a deeper level. I know these revolutionary truths can radically transform hurting marriages and make healthy marriages even stronger."

—Robert Morris, founding senior pastor, Gateway Church;
bestselling author of *The Blessed Life*, *Truly Free*, and *Frequency*

"Tested, real-world marriage help meets behavioral science and biology. If you've been looking for something that can help you create the marriage of your dreams, look no further."

—John C. Maxwell, #1 *New York Times* bestselling
author, coach, and speaker

"Over the last decade, the StrengthsFinder assessment has transformed the worlds of business and leadership. In this book, Evans and Kelsey apply these findings to marriage, and the results are fantastic."

—Dr. Henry Cloud, clinical psychologist, acclaimed
leadership expert, and bestselling author

STRENGTHS BASED MARRIAGE

BUILD A STRONGER RELATIONSHIP BY UNDERSTANDING EACH OTHER'S GIFTS

JIMMY EVANS & ALLAN KELSEY

NELSON
BOOKS

An Imprint of Thomas Nelson

Published in Nashville, Tennessee, by Nelson Books, an imprint of Thomas Nelson. Nelson Books and Thomas Nelson are registered trademarks of HarperCollins Christian Publishing, Inc.

Thomas Nelson titles may be purchased in bulk for educational, business, fund-raising, or sales promotional use. For information, please e-mail SpecialMarkets@ThomasNelson.com.

Unless otherwise noted, scripture quotations are from THE NEW KING JAMES VERSION®. © 1982 by Thomas Nelson, Inc. Used by permission. All rights reserved.

Scriptures marked NASB are from the NEW AMERICAN STANDARD BIBLE®, © The Lockman Foundation 1960, 1962, 1963, 1968, 1971, 1972, 1973, 1975, 1977, 1995. Used by permission.

Scriptures marked NIV are from the Holy Bible, New International Version®, NIV® Copyright ©1973, 1978, 1984, 2011 by Biblica, Inc.® Used by permission. All rights reserved worldwide.

The non-Gallup information you are receiving has not been approved and is not sanctioned or endorsed by Gallup in any way. Opinions, views, and interpretations of StrengthsFinder results are solely the beliefs of Jimmy Evans and Allan Kelsey.

Gallup®, Clifton StrengthsFinder®, StrengthsFinder®, and the 34 Clifton StrengthsFinder® theme names are trademarks of Gallup, Inc. All rights reserved.

Library of Congress Cataloging-in-Publication Data

Names: Evans, Jimmy, author.
Title: Strengths based marriage : build a stronger relationship by understanding each other's gifts / Jimmy Evans and Allan Kelsey.
Description: Nashville : Thomas Nelson, 2016. | Includes bibliographical references.
Identifiers: LCCN 2016017800 | ISBN 9780718083625
Subjects: LCSH: Marriage--Religious aspects--Christianity.
Classification: LCC BV835 .E8855 2016 | DDC 248.8/44--dc23 LC record available at https://lccn.loc.gov/2016017800

Printed in the United States of America

17 18 19 20 RRD 6

We dedicate this book to every couple who has suffered relationally from avoidable pain caused by a lack of knowledge of each other. Our prayer is that you will find understanding and peace and fall deeper in love through the revelation in this book.

CONTENTS

CONTENTS

AUTHORS' NOTE

This book has the power to strongly transform your marriage, regardless of its current condition. We suggest you approach this book similarly to how you should approach marriage: the more you put into it, the more you will get out of it.

You will encounter the voices of two experts, Jimmy Evans and Allan Kelsey, who speak to the most frequent marital challenges and to corresponding opportunities for growth. Each chapter deals with a specific marriage topic by looking at it from the perspective of a marriage expert (Jimmy) as well as from that of a strengths expert (Allan). By bringing together these two areas of expertise, *Strengths Based Marriage* offers a unique approach to understanding yourself, your spouse, and the mystery of marriage.

To make the most of this book, you and your spouse will need to take the Clifton StrengthsFinder® assessment. We'll provide you with a link to the assessment later in the book. With your assessment results in hand and the guidance of this book, you can experience a level of intimacy and strength of relationship that will transform your marriage forever.

STRENGTHS BASED MARRIAGE VIDEO SESSIONS

Experience the *Strengths Based Marriage* video sessions featuring more than two hours of exclusive video content with marriage authority Jimmy Evans, Strengths Coach Allan Kelsey, and the testimonies of other couples who have seen their marriages renewed and reignited.

Through these *Strengths Based Marriage* videos, accessible online, you'll discover how to apply the life-changing knowledge of your strengths and reach the full potential in your relationship. (More information follows the About the Authors section at the back of the book.)

INTRODUCTION

The Empathy® Story

Allan Kelsey, Strengths Expert

John came to me because he was having trouble being understood at work and wanted to know how to communicate his perspective and ideas better. Additionally, he said that while his marriage was good, lately he and his wife had felt distant and weren't connecting quite the way they used to. They had been married five years.

His wife, Susan, had taken Gallup's Clifton StrengthsFinder® assessment and was encouraging him to do so, but he didn't understand why she was making such a big deal about it. Susan spoke frequently about her results and wanted to see him through the strengths lens so she could understand him better. She told him that it would help him at work to know his strengths, so John finally agreed. He took the assessment, then came to see me with his results.

When taking the strengths assessment, there are two sets of results available:

- Top five strengths. This is the first option available from the website, and it reveals the top five strengths in descending order.
- Full thirty-four strengths. The second option allows the candidates to know all thirty-four of their strengths in descending order.

As a Strengths Coach, I had asked John to choose the second option and bring me his results so we could look at his top-ten and bottom-five strengths together.

A good Clifton StrengthsFinder®–based development plan involves focusing on the strong parts of your life—the eight or ten strengths at the top of your list—as well as being aware of the softer strengths at the bottom of your list, because it's there that challenges can be present if the person is not aware of those strengths.

John and I worked on a great plan using his strengths for work, and near the end of our time together we looked over the strengths appearing lower on his list. As it turns out, the strength of Empathy® was number thirty-three out of thirty-four on his list. Ordinarily I would have told him that since this was among his bottom-five strengths, he should be aware of it and work to ensure that this result wouldn't hinder his interactions with others. But this was no ordinary situation: I knew Susan had Empathy® in her top five. That changed everything.

As we talked about his low Empathy® score, he told me how he never intended to lack Empathy®. He said, "If you leave me to my own devices, just walking down the street, I typically don't display an empathetic perspective. It just doesn't come to me.

I'm not trying to avoid it; it's just not on my radar. I understand Empathy®, and I try to live with it in my life. When someone tells me something sad, I like to respond empathetically, but it comes from a processed decision, not a natural 'I can't help myself' kind of place."

Then we turned our conversation to Susan. She had Empathy® among her top-five strengths, meaning it is a very strong part of her everyday life. She cannot function without demonstrating Empathy®; it's just who she is. Every day she feels what others feel. Every day she senses the deep emotional condition of others and is often able to articulate just how they feel—sometimes even before they can. John told me this trait was one of the things that attracted him to her in the first place.

I quickly helped John see that just by doing life his normal way, he was giving off an unspoken yet subtle message to everyone around him that said, "Empathy® doesn't factor in my world and has no place in my life." For Susan, on the other hand, an empathetic approach to life isn't a choice to make—it's who she is. Empathy® is a critical part of how she evaluates everything, the lens through which she sees the world.

When you put those two factors together, you can see that John was sending a message that said, "I don't see Empathy®," which Susan interpreted as, "I don't see you." Put another way, John's message—"Your way of operating doesn't factor naturally into my world"—became "*You* don't factor in my world." Or even worse, "I don't typically make room for Empathy®," translated to "I don't typically make room for you."

John was devastated. He was unaware that his bottom-five strengths were having such a crushing effect on his wife's heart.

He began to cry. He told me how much he loved her and that he was so sad to have been hurting her all this time without even knowing it. We talked awhile longer, and after a little time he told me he had a plan to fix this problem.

The next morning at ten, John decided to take the rest of the day off and called Susan at work. He asked her to request emergency time off for the rest of the day and to meet him at the local outdoor mall.

It was a beautiful spring day, and they met at the fountain in the middle of the mall. Susan was very anxious. This kind of activity was not normal for John. She wondered if he had been fired or laid off, or worse—had someone died? John took her hands and led her to a park bench. As they sat in the warm spring sunshine, this is what John said.

"I know you have Empathy® as one of your top strengths. I have learned some new things about all this lately, and I want you to know that I am so sorry I have been hurting you. All this time I have been doing life the way I normally do, not know-ing that I have been inadvertently sending a message every day that, to you, probably sounds like: 'I don't see you, how you feel doesn't matter to me, and I don't care.' Darling, I want you to know, I am so sorry."

Susan started to cry. John had more to say, but it didn't matter.

She kept crying. He reached out to her, and she put her arms around him and cried some more.

After she composed herself, she looked him straight in the eyes and said: "For the first time in our marriage, since the day we said I do, I feel seen by you." And then she cried some more.

John and Susan spent more time on the park bench that morning. They talked about their love and their communication. They talked about their future, and they renewed their commitment to each other, to see each other through the lens of what is best. Later, John told me that the rest of that day felt like a scene from a romance novel. They walked hand in hand, he bought her a spring dress, they ate leisurely, and time passed at their pace. It was magical.

Years later I asked John how his relationship with Susan was going, and he said: "Allan, that single spring day did more to deepen and advance our marriage, more to heal our relationship, and more to strengthen our communication than anything else we have encountered. I could not be more grateful. It has established a language for our relationship that is present to this day, and I can't imagine where we would be without it."

My heartfelt prayer is that you, too, will find revelatory insight throughout this book, and that your marriage and other relationships will take on a new dimension of empowerment.

INTRODUCTION TO STRENGTHS

STRENGTHS BACKGROUND

Allan Kelsey, Strengths Expert

The genesis of something always matters because the beginning of a journey inevitably colors what the rest of the journey will look like. The seed of something determines what will sprout from it later, so beginnings matter. The origin story of the strengths movement will give you some background and help reveal why it will be an important tool for your personal discovery and for your marriage.

Let us begin with an account popularly referenced by the Strengths Coaches at the Gallup® organization.[1] The head of a school had concerns during the 1950s about students' reading retention and asked for the incoming freshmen to be tested. He wanted to know how fast they could read while retaining at least 80 percent of the content.

The professors tested the students and learned that most students were reading about 90 words per minute and retaining 80 percent of what they read. A small portion of the students, however, were reading around 350 words per minute and also retaining 80 percent of the content. Now, let us put that into a little context. Most books have between 10 and 11 words per line and 20 to 25 lines on a page, meaning most books have between 225 and 275 words on a page. That means the bulk of the students were reading less than a half page in a minute and retaining 80 percent, while a small portion were reading a full page and a half in a minute and retaining most of what they had read.

After the professors had reported their findings, they decided to put both groups of readers through six weeks of speed-reading courses and then test them again to see what would happen. As the weeks went by, the test administrators began to form their own little pockets of expectation. Some predicted that the students reading 90 words per minute were going to improve significantly, while those reading 350 words per minute would improve less because they were already reading pretty fast.

A second group of administrators also believed that the students reading 90 words per minute would show improvement, but they felt that the 350s were already reading as fast as they could. They predicted no more than 1 or 2 percentage points of improvement for the fast readers. A third group of administrators agreed that the students reading 90 words per minute would improve, but they expected the 350s to actually get worse based on a psychology principle known as "unconscious competence." Unconscious competence is just a fancy way of saying that when people are performing at a high level and are then made aware of their skill, they get nervous and their performance worsens.

After six weeks of speed-reading training, the results were tabulated. The students who had been reading 90 words per minute increased to 140 words per minute—a 60 percent improvement. But the next set of results was stunning: The students who had been reading 350 words per minute jumped to roughly 2,900 words per minute. Their reading pace absolutely shot through the roof. The students were reading 9 to 11 pages in a minute and retaining 80 percent of what they had read. The professors were baffled by the results. But they quickly agreed that something significant had been discovered about what people are capable of.

To be sure, reading roughly 10 pages in a minute and retaining 80 percent of what you have read is impressive! But a bigger point existed amid this discovery. The students who were reading 350 words per minute had been talented readers from the very start. They'd had a talent for reading before even being tested, but in all likelihood, they themselves did not know it. The study's findings prompted two questions: Do other talents exist that we don't know about? And is it possible to identify those talents specifically?

HUNTING FOR TALENT

In an effort to discover areas of talent or true strength, a survey was designed with approximately two thousand questions. The survey was given to the highest achieving people in very diverse fields of endeavor, because the search was on to find the best of what people have to offer. NBA basketball players, hotel cleaners, airline technicians, doctors, dentists, lawyers, and others were all given a chance to be screened for impressive, repeatable talent.

The assessment was distributed around the world and administered over a forty-year period. The hunt for talent had begun.

Talents are not abilities, such as a phenomenal golf swing or an amazing knowledge of stingrays; rather, they are inherent traits. These traits are uniquely, instinctively, and permanently yours. They are not just things you do but rather repeatable ways you see and approach life. In short, they help to make up who you are.

ADDRESSING "WEAKNESS FIXING"

The two-thousand-question survey and its results helped contribute to the creation of the current Clifton StrengthsFinder® assessment, which reveals thirty-four talents as they occur in every human being. They occur in a unique sequence, revealing first the strongest or most dominant talents in your life. As the list progresses, the level of natural strength in each talent diminishes.[2]

In the early days of the survey, people began to follow a somewhat predictable pattern after discovering their results: They would spend time looking at their number-one talent in order to understand it, then do the same with number two, then numbers three and four, spending less and less time with each trait. Somewhere around result number five, participants began skipping the middle-range results and going straight to number thirty-four—the last talent on their list—and looking at the ones that are least strong and spending time there. This was puzzling. Why focus on the weakest abilities when looking at results from a survey designed to find strengths?

When asked why they showed so much interest in their lowest scores, people replied with consistency: "If I am going to get the promotion, get the job, or get the girl, I have to fix where I am broken. I have to shore up or strengthen my weaknesses. You just showed me where I am not so strong. So, thanks a lot! I'm going to focus there and try to fix it." After watching the participants focus on their lowest results from the assessment, some very significant findings emerged.

First, it is possible to improve the rank of a particular talent that is low on your list of thirty-four talents. By dedicating effort to improving that talent, you can improve your lowest talent (which in my case happens to be the strength of Empathy®) and its position by roughly five to seven points. Hypothetically, I could move Empathy® from talent position thirty-four up to twenty-seven. But in doing so, what have I really done? The talent is never going to be in my top five, so moving it up marginally seems like a less than efficient way to spend my time.

Second, if I pour all that energy into improving my Empathy® ranking, nothing is happening where I am strongest. All my focus is being spent where I have the least capacity. This approach is certainly not the best use of my time. Furthermore, while this low Empathy® talent of mine can remain five to seven points elevated as long as I focus on it, the minute I stop my efforts, the talent repositions itself to its natural, lower ranking. From these observations, it seems there is little value to be gained from focusing on the talents at the bottom of my list.

These insights have come from observing people's behavior, but what scientific explanations support the idea of innate talent and the creation of it in the brain? Such information would potentially support the idea that people are not able to permanently and significantly improve their lower-ranking Clifton StrengthsFinder® talents. With the help of some brain experts, here are some of my explanations (in layman's terms) concerning recent discoveries about talent in the brain.

IT IS ALL IN THE BRAIN

Let's take a look at the formation of connections in the brain during early development in order to understand our natural leanings. Forty-two days after conception, you are the size of a postage stamp in the womb. It is around this point that brain development begins, and for the next 120 days, that is primarily what is being built. By the end of the next 120 days—at an impressive rate of ninety-five hundred neuron constructions per second—your brain is already a gray blob with a hundred billion neuron intersections. These intersections are called nodes or neurons, and each neuron must connect with another neuron. These neurons are connected with a "string" called an axon, and once a connection is made, a pathway exists between two neuron points through which ideas can flow. Neuron connectors are also called synapses, and they map the nebula of the brain. The human brain contains billions of neurons, and each one makes about fifteen thousand connections. It is staggering to think about how the formative neuron-mapping process of the brain is complete by around age three.

The point of this short biology lesson is simply to illustrate that these connections exist; and some of them, for whatever reason, flow information better than others. If it were possible for us to somehow look into my brain while it is being used, we would find the equivalent of a huge tangled ball of wiring with millions of connections. Some connections in my brain are small and light and cannot deal with much traffic. These connections are like drinking straws: small and thin, capable of transporting fluid (or ideas), but not very effectively. Other connections are thicker, like garden hoses, capable of flowing much more information. Finally, you have the thickest connections in the brain, which are like the hoses that connect to fire hydrants. When you open up a thick connection, huge volumes of information can flow through it in the blink of an eye.

If we were to take out my thickest axon connection, then roll it over to see what is written on the bottom, it would say—written in God's handwriting—the word *Achiever*® (my number one Clifton StrengthsFinder® talent). In other words, that strong connection developed during my formative years.

Fact is, we have talents hardwired into our brains, and we were created that way on purpose. There is a biological reason the straw-size connection at position number thirty-four on your talent list cannot transport as much information as the fire hose–size connection at number one on your list. That's why it is not productive to focus on making the lower talents on the list perform like the stronger talents. There is just no way as much fluid can flow through a straw as through a fire hose! Similarly, there is no way Empathy® (which is lowest on my list of talents) will ever function as strongly as Achiever® (which is highest on my talent list). It could be said that there is a biological reason for why that will just never happen for me.

Some people might say that having a low Empathy® score is a negative hurdle I should actively try to jump. It is very true that having low Empathy® on my Clifton StrengthsFinder® list does not give me a license to be overly rigid toward people. I don't get to say, "Suck it up, cupcake," or be grossly insensitive just because my Empathy® ranking is low (even though I have been tempted to).

These talents are subject to my decisions and my governance. With this knowledge, I know that I will never be as great at Empathy® as others who have it in their top five, so I can stop trying to compete with them. There is no need to feel miserable about my failure to measure up. I find this very liberating. I can instead focus on the things that I *am* actually good at, where I have true and measurable talent, and get busy improving those. After all, it's where I have the greatest potential and where some of my strongest contributions will likely come from.

YOU ARE UNIQUE!

What is the point of all this information? The point is that knowing where you have talent equips you to do something about it. For the rest of your life, whether you do something about it or not, you will have superior ability around your particular mix of strongest talents (the top-five talents on your Clifton StrengthsFinder® Assessment). It would be a shame if your talents equipped you to read 2,900 words-per-minute, but you did not even know it. In order to know what your strongest talents are, you need them to be succinctly and objectively identified.

Every one of us has the ability to produce world-class results in our lives because of the talents we have. What stops you is simply not knowing what they are. How can you do something with your strengths if you don't know you have that kind of capacity?

You have to find out where you are strong, where you are talented, and what tools God has given you so you can do something with them. That is the whole point of this exercise.

Remember, this is not just about what you do. It is about who you are. There is a difference. Consider the following example: I can type on the computer, swing a golf club, or spend time with my kids. Those are three separate and distinctly different activities; they have nothing to do with each other. There is, however, one thing common among all of them: me. *I* type on the computer. *I* take who *I* am and go play golf or spend time with my kids. I am the one who is doing it, so what I do comes out of who I am. All too often, we try to correct *what* we are doing instead of first working to understand *who* we are. But it is only after we uncover *who* we are that we can understand *what* we do. That creates a far more aligned balance for our lives and brings our daily actions closer to our true identities and the place of our strongest contribution.

Finally, you may ask,

> SIMPLY ADDING INTENTIONAL SKILL, EXPERIENCE, OR KNOWLEDGE TO THE TOP AREAS OF TALENT ON YOUR LIST WILL TRANSFORM YOUR 350-WORDS-PER-MINUTE TALENT TO A 2,900-WORDS-PER-MINUTE STRENGTH.

"Doesn't everybody have these talents? How many other people in the world can do what I do? How many other people are just like me?"

Let's answer this by asking a question: How many people would you need to talk to in order to find *one other person* with the same five Clifton StrengthsFinder® results as you, with the exact same talent sequence? The answer is roughly thirty-three million. The world population is expected to exceed 7.4 billion in 2017. If you do the math, that means there are fewer than 225 people who have the same five talents in your sequence. These people could include a little Australian Aborigine child, an old Malaysian guy, a Canadian housewife, or an African businessman. That statistic holds up all over the world, regardless of race, religious denomination, gender, or culture. Our talents transcend demographics. One person in thirty-three million is a pretty rare occurrence, I must say.

What if we looked for one person with the same top *six* talents as you, in the same order? There are barely enough people on the planet to find *one* person who shares your same top six. From here, statistically, it starts to get crazy. To find one person who has the same top eight talents in your order the number is somewhere in the region of seven hundred billion people. You get the picture. You are incredibly unique—irreplaceably unique. Remember, too, that this is not all of who you are. If you imagine yourself as a pie chart, then today we are just dealing with one slice: the Clifton StrengthsFinder® piece.

So what is the point? The point is, there is nobody else like you. Furthermore, not only is there nobody just like you on the planet today, but never has there been anyone like you in the history of time. And in case you were wondering, it is highly unlikely that there could be anyone just like you in the future. We now have statistical proof to show it.

This understanding has two important implications. First, if nobody else is like you, then who is your competition? Just think about that question for a minute.

You are completely unique. No one else can "do you" because every human is so irreplaceably one-of-a-kind. We can all take a deep breath and let go of any anxiety that someone else will come along to replace us. If nobody can "do me," then there really is a place for me and for what I uniquely bring to the world.

Second, if you choose not to show up to a commitment you have made, is that really a problem? Yes, because no one else can replicate your identity. No one else can do you, so your contribution would be missed if you didn't show up.

There is an accountability that comes with the unique ability that God has given you and me.

IT'S ABOUT YOUR JOY

Another important reason for knowing your strengths and using them daily is because it just feels fantastic to do so. Remember when we were in my brain, poking around for the thickest connection that flows the most information? While the scientists were in there, they also found that there are glands in the brain that release an enzyme that rushes throughout the brain and makes you feel incredible. This kind of natural buzz occurs when you use your strengths. Isn't that amazing? As humans, we are rewarded with a legal, biological buzz when we exercise our talents. Here are some of the outward signals or physical "tells" that your brain is being influenced by that enzyme.

Imagine you are at an event, listening to a talk or lecture. The speaker exhibits raised eyebrows, and you notice the person really leaning into the message, using hand gestures and huge variations in voice pitch and tone. You can tell the speaker is completely engaged in what is going on in the room, and after a while, he is amazed at how quickly time has passed. These are all signs that the speaker's brain is being fed by the energizing enzymes that show that talent is in use. You feel this way when you function within your strengths, when you do what you do best.

As a result, we keep going back to where we feel strong because it feels good. When it feels good, we want more. The more we do what we are great at, the better we become; and the better we become, the more others benefit from it. In the meantime, though, we get more joy from exercising our strengths. It becomes a self-sustaining cycle of positive contribution and reward.

Your strengths are built in, and they are designed for your best, one-of-a-kind contribution. For the most part, strengths are neutral, meaning they don't make you do good or bad things. They could be described as amplifiers. I could drive my strengths through a lens of broken character in my life, and the effect would be amplified brokenness on the other side. On the other hand, I could drive my strengths through strong or good character, and the result would be amplified goodness or helpfulness on the other side. It's my choice.

Now that you know more about these strengths, where they came from, and how they apply in your life, we suggest that you each take your Clifton StrengthsFinder® assessment now. You will find it at www.gallupstrengthscenter.com. As a couple, you will get the most out of this book if you both take the Clifton StrengthsFinder® assessment.

Enter both your and your spouse's Clifton StrengthsFinder® results on a chart similar to the one following and keep the chart handy for easy future reference.

CLIFTON STRENGTHSFINDER® RESULTS	
HIS	HERS
1.	1.
2.	2.
3.	3.
4.	4.
5.	5.

COUNTERFEITS

Allan Kelsey, Strengths Expert

The big idea behind the counterfeit principle is simply this: every talent has a counterfeit. It's not an opposite; it's a counterfeit. It's like the dark shadow of a strength. It proves that the strengths are actually there, but its effect is not positive or good. This counterfeit is typically a hurtful or destructive behavior that is deceptively associated with a particular Clifton StrengthsFinder® talent. Every time we allow the presence of a counterfeit in our lives, it produces fruit that can be counterproductive or even destructive. This is the dark side to the strengths conversation we are aware of, but we have not had the language to describe it. The whole trap of talent counterfeits is designed to lock us behind a false and destructive understanding of our talents and to thereby neutralize them.

Now, before we get further down the road, I want to establish what I mean by the words *talent* and *strength* so we all can be on the same page. The Clifton StrengthsFinder® assessment reveals talent in our lives. *Talent* is the word we use to describe latent potential. It's the word we use when we see a twelve-year-old playing with a ball in an open field. After observing him or her for a few minutes, we might say, "Boy, that kid has talent." What we mean is, that kid has loads of potential even if it is not quite a strength yet. Talent in its raw form, if left undeveloped, could provide a marginal advantage over others, but is not yet a true strength.

Furthermore, it is not acceptable for the expression of a talent to be hurtful or destructive to you or the people around you. If it is, then it is not a burgeoning strength at all. Only talent made stronger through skill, experience, or knowledge, then applied in health and balance for you and for those around you, can become a strength.

> **FOR A TALENT TO BECOME A TRUE STRENGTH, IT IS NECESSARY TO INTENTIONALLY ADD SKILL, EXPERIENCE, OR KNOWLEDGE TO THAT TALENT.**

I make this qualification because it doesn't make sense to attribute the word *strength*—which has power and value connotations—to an action that is ultimately destructive to you or to those around you. To clarify, then: *Talent* is ability in raw, unpolished form. *Strength* is talent in use, but polished for purpose and beneficial to you and those around you. Now, let's get back to the explanation of talent counterfeits.

The nuanced nature of talent counterfeits is what makes them so sneaky and hard to find. They hide in plain sight.

Because of their deceptive nature, we rarely have the clarity or language to describe them. A counterfeit is like a Trojan horse of sorts. On the surface it appears to be a gift, and it even comes from people whom we love and trust. However, once we accept it, once the individual has absorbed it, the counterfeit can destroy the individual from the inside.

WHAT IS A TALENT COUNTERFEIT?

Let's use my number-one talent as an example: Achiever®.

To understand the counterfeit, I must first know the real thing. So let me tell you the truth about my Achiever® strength. In my heart, at the root of my Achiever® strength, I just love to get stuff done. I am highly productive and get a sense of energy from accomplishing things. I like to make lists of the things I need to accomplish, and while often those lists are just in my head, sometimes I write them down. Occasionally I will get something done that is not on one of my lists. When that happens, it's not unusual for me to complete the task, then add it to my list just so I can check it off. *Yeaahh!* I just love the feeling of accomplishment. This represents the truth about the Achiever® in me.

Now let's look at my Achiever® counterfeit. As others watch me, it might be easy for them to conclude the following: "Doing stuff is more important to Allan than connecting with people. He values task accomplishment more highly than he does people." One individual could make that observation, make a label for me, and stick it on my back. Then in conversation he might bring it up with a friend and mention his perception of me. He might say, "You know, I've noticed that Allan is always so busy. It sure doesn't seem like he makes much time for people. What do you think?"

At this point, the friend might consider what she sees and come to the same conclusion based on her observations. Now there are two people who are in agreement about me. They have collaborated their observations and through confirmation can establish their facts. Together they have created the "Allan is less interested in people" label and stuck it on me. And just like that, an attribution error has been born. To them their statement is factual because they have observed proof to back it up. Their observed facts have some strong traction and are hard to refute. The damage has already been done.

THE DIFFERENCE BETWEEN TRUTH AND FACTS

In college I studied epistemology, the study of how we know what we know. Doing so helped me to see there is a discernable difference between truth and facts.

For the sake of today's discussion, let's assume the following definitions for these two words: *Truth*, in its purest form, is that which is collectively and objectively correct and right. It speaks not only to action, but also to motivation. It gets to the heart of the matter. An example of a true statement would be: *When he said, "I love you," we all knew it to be true.*

In this statement, we identify the truth as being at least two things: 1) that he does, in fact, have the feelings and commitment that we call love for her; and 2) that his statement to her is not manipulative but reflective of how he genuinely feels. Statement and intentions align.

A fact, on the other hand, is correctness that we assign to a situation based on data, science, or observation. An example of a factual statement would be: *after analyzing the X-ray, the doctor pointed to the lung cancer in the patient.*

In this situation, facts are honest, but they are based on the externally observed evidence alone. It is factual that science has pointed to the evidence of lung cancer in the patient. We could say, "The facts show that he has lung cancer," and we would not be amiss in making that statement.

In short, we could say: truth speaks to *that which is,* and facts acknowledge *that which we can observe or prove.*

Now let's look at how the facts and the truth are not the same thing. I might go to a party and—knowing my wife needs me to be extra friendly for this group of people—put on a smile and behave as if I'm having a good time. It's a choice I make to present an "I'm having fun" face, when in truth, on the inside, I am not really having that much fun and I would rather not be there. If you polled the attendees at the party and asked them, "Is Allan having fun?" they would say yes. In this case, the factual evidence as confirmed by the partygoers supports this fact: *Allan is having fun at the party.* If you want the truth, though, you would have to ask me if I'm really having fun. Honestly, those types of parties are not always the most fun for me.

The facts and the truth do not always line up. In fact, this happens to us on many levels every day. There is a tension between the truth and the facts, and it presents an interesting opportunity to those of us who identify it.

The tension of these two realities sets up an opportunity for you and me to choose which reality we will agree with. Will we choose to agree with the truth of a matter or the facts of a matter? Simply put, the product of this tension between truth and facts is *choice*!

This concept of choice plays very strongly into the counterfeits principle. In our lives and in our strengths based conversation, your talent and how it will become a helpful expression in your life is the *truth*. When other people incorrectly label your talent based on the observable behavior they see in you, those labels are merely the *facts*. Modern science has called this false labeling a *fundamental attribution error.*[1] To return to my party example, though the partygoers believe their observations are accurate, what they have determined is actually an *error.*

HOW DOES A TALENT COUNTERFEIT WORK, EXACTLY?

The whole purpose of this illustration is to point out the tension between truth and facts. Every day we get the opportunity to choose one idea over another, to align with either the facts of our lives or the truth of our lives. It is our choice.

Talent counterfeits live off the same principle. The truth is, we have talents. These talents are given to us for good in our lives and in the lives of others around us. However, the way others observe that truth causes them to make a label—an assumptive label—about what our motivations are, and they stick that label on us. When others watch us and decide what our behavior means, their *facts* conflict with the *truth* of our strengths, resulting in a fundamental attribution error.

This is where the talent counterfeit comes in, because your behavior solicits a label from people who have based their facts on behavior that is quite obvious to them. Since their label is based on observable behavior—on facts—the label is difficult to refute. People may draw a conclusion about you, but the truth about what is going on in your heart is often different. And in terms of talents, your heart is where the truth about your talents is purest. As a result, facts don't often reflect the truth. It's all so subtle, yet so real.

WHERE ALL THE DAMAGE IS DONE

Eventually I learned that people think this way about me. They believe that as an Achiever®, I care less about people and more about getting stuff done. At first, this idea was just annoying to me, and I would simply dismiss it. But over time I heard it quite often. The problem is: *This counterfeit idea was fed to me by the people I love and trust the most. It could come to me from my parents, from my brothers, or even from my pastor.*

The people who love me mean well, and of course they only point it out to help me grow. After all, if you knew someone was hurting himself or others with his behavior, wouldn't you want to talk to him about it? Of course you would. Over the years I have repeatedly heard Achiever® counterfeit phrases that contain all kinds of words, and they all boil down to the idea that I am less interested in people and just want to accomplish stuff.

Eventually this became too much to ignore, and as any self-aware individual would do, I began searching my soul and investigating the accusations. Here's the dialogue with myself that resulted:

I hear people tell me all the time that I am more interested in getting stuff done than connecting with people. I know that is not true, but that's what they say. I am sort of busy, but I like getting stuff done, and I'm really good at it. I feel great when things are accomplished and when we are moving forward, but not at the expense of other people. My mom said it to me just the other day, though. There must be something to this. I've heard it so often.

Okay, I'm not going to be accused of this anymore. I don't like that people think this about me because it is not true. I will show them it's not true. They only say this about me because of my Achiever® strength. So, to stop the accusation, I will stop the source: my Achiever®. I will stop achieving so much and focus more on people. All right! That settles it. I now have a plan to help others see that I am interested in people. My plan is to oppose and undo the thing that makes people say I'm not interested in people. I will oppose my Achiever®.

The Achiever® counterfeit has entered like a Trojan horse, and the pain of buying into a lie is about to begin. Can you see how devastating this is? Even though I have been given an amazing Achiever® ability that drives my most significant contribution to the world, I am going to turn against the very thing God gave me for good by trying to shut it down. All this is in response to a counterfeit. The facts of the counterfeit are not the truth, but I have allowed the label placed on me by others to crush the truth in my life. The saddest part is, now I am doing it to myself.

The second issue here is that I have now turned against my intrinsic source of energy, power, and motivation. If I turn against it to shut it down, it's a little like using a serving tray to shut off a fountainhead. I can push down on the fountain outlet all I like, but water will continue coming out of the ground. That is what our Clifton StrengthsFinder® strengths are like:

fountains of eternal contribution. I don't know if you have ever tried shutting off a fountainhead with a serving tray. I haven't, but if it is anything like trying to stop a garden sprinkler, then I can tell you from personal experience it can't be done. You cannot effectively and permanently shut off the power of your talent. Furthermore, while you are busy trying to do that, it consumes your time. Nothing effective can happen anywhere else in your life because that fruitless action is too demanding of your time and focus. Even if you turn against your talent, it cannot be effectively eliminated, and while you are busy trying to shut it down, very little of value is getting done elsewhere.

What is the point?

The point is, we tend to speak these counterfeits over each other all the time, whether we mean to or not. I don't even have to know anything about Clifton StrengthsFinder® talents to identify a counterfeit in your life. We simply observe each other and name what appear to be facts all the time. But by doing so, we are routinely and repeatedly provoking each other to move away from the truth, away from the strongest contributions of our lives. This can be incredibly destructive to people and to marriages.

Instead, we should learn the truth about each other by understanding each other's strengths. If we know each other's strengths, we can call each other up to the greatness of what we can be instead of destroying each other by agreeing with counterfeits that tear us down.

Counterfeits are easy to observe in each other and even easier to reinforce. It will take an act of your will to identify the counterfeits in your life and in the life of your spouse, replace that language with a strengths language, and retrain yourselves to speak the truth over each other. Fortunately, the antidote for a counterfeit is simple and universal; it is open transparency. Simply open your heart and speak transparently about your real motivations and emotions. Help others understand the "why" behind your actions and redirect the incorrect attribution that is placed on you.

If you do this, I am convinced—because I have seen it in my own marriage—that your marriage and your relationships in general will undergo a strengths makeover. You will become talent scouts, hunting for what is best in each other and using the strengths language that so accurately allows you to encourage each other toward the best of what you are and who you can become!

STOPPING THE CYCLES OF PAIN

THREE

THE PAIN DANCE

Jimmy Evans, Marriage Expert

My wife, Karen, and I have been married for more than forty years. We have two married children and five beautiful grandchildren to show for it. We have a great marriage and are very thankful for that. But it wasn't always this way.

After several years of marriage, we were on the brink of divorce. We married at age nineteen after several years of rocky dating. One week before we got married, Karen told me she wouldn't marry me because of how immoral I was. But I promised to change (and did), and we followed through with our wedding.

Shortly thereafter, the fireworks started, and our fights took a turn for the worse. If you had asked me back then why we fought so much, I would have told you it was because I married the weirdest woman on earth. She was beautiful—but weird. And she was my opposite in almost every category.

If you asked me today why we fought so much, I would say it was because of ignorance. Back then I thought Karen was weird and she thought the same of me. We fought because we didn't understand each other. We also fought because we were in a battle to change each other.

There is an old joke about marriage that goes like this: "Marriage is about becoming one. The question is, which one?" Ouch! That is too true. It was surely true of us for the first years of our marriage. I felt that I was normal, and because Karen wasn't like me, she wasn't normal. It was a pretty simple formula, and my job was to shame her, scold her, lecture her, and educate her until she became normal like me.

The problem was, she just didn't train well. At least that is what I thought at the time. To make matters worse Karen did the exact same thing to me. She rejected my differences and did everything she could to change me to be like her—which, in her mind, would make me normal. But I despised it and so did she. And every time it happened we damaged and demeaned each other more.

Finally we found ourselves one dark night in a yelling match in the middle of the living room. I pointed my finger in her face and told her to get out of the house and out of my life. That was the low point in our marriage. I didn't want to lose her, but I also didn't know how to keep her. In fact, I was afraid of what was going to happen if our fights continued to escalate.

So what changed? What happened that stopped the pain dance and caused our marriage to be healthy? First of all, I dedicated our marriage and myself to God and apologized to Karen for being such a jerk. That made a huge difference. But second, we began to embrace our differences and realized they were God-given.

We came into marriage with the very destructive belief that compatibility meant sameness and that lie caused us to do deep damage to each other and almost destroyed our marriage. We were locked in a dangerous dance. I would see something in Karen that was different from me, and I didn't understand. I would reject her and verbally lash out at her. She would get hurt and retaliate both to defend herself and to correct me. I also felt rejected and wounded by her words and actions. And we danced . . . and danced . . . and danced . . . until we were worn out, wounded, and ready to throw in the towel.

Today we realize that we are different by God's design. Rather than reject and correct each other, we accept and love each other. And more than anything else, we understand our differences and realize they make our marriage more dynamic. We are two halves of a whole. We complete each other. We are better together.

One of the reasons I have been so excited about writing this book with Allan Kelsey is to empower couples to really understand and respect their differences. If Karen and I had understood each other's strengths and differences, it would have totally changed our marriage in the early years. It wouldn't have just stopped our fights; it would have led to acceptance, cooperation, and affirmation. That is the exact opposite of what we experienced.

Are you in a pain dance? Now that you have taken your assessment and know your strengths (and hopefully also your spouse's), you are poised to take the first step to change everything. And it begins by accepting and honoring the inherent differences in your spouse.

This isn't to say that nothing about your spouse or marriage needs to change. But it is to say that the surest way to fail is to try to change an unchangeable. And the truth is, you and your spouse are different by God's design. As you read through this book we will reveal many of the ways you are different from your spouse. We will give you some important keys to understanding each other, meeting each other's needs, and truly enjoying the journey of marriage.

Allan will be explaining the dynamic of your strengths—how to understand them and how they work together to complement and connect you. Allan is truly an expert in the field of strengths training. He, more than anyone else, has helped Karen and me to understand our differences and to know how to use that knowledge to relate to each other intimately and intelligently.

That is what we want for you. By the end of this book we want you and your marriage to be changed. If you are in a pain dance, we want it to turn into a happy dance. Your marriage can become what you dreamed it would be. There is nothing like understanding to empower us for success.

Allan Kelsey, Strengths Expert

Jimmy's story about his marriage is not a unique one. Many of us have stories like his, which start with pain and misunderstanding. But unlike Jimmy and Karen—who have had four decades to work on their marriage—we don't have their expert tools and we need another way to see each other. I truly believe if Karen and Jimmy had learned the Clifton StrengthsFinder® language to understand each other earlier in their marriage, they would have saved themselves years of heartache. So, as a way of rewinding time, why don't we go back to their early days and take a look at their marriage and interactions through the lens of their Clifton StrengthsFinder® results? Here are Karen's and Jimmy's top and bottom strengths:

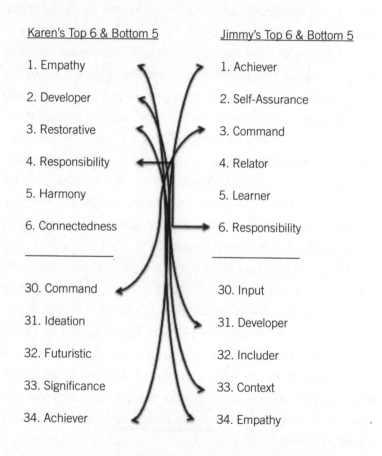

Karen's Top 6 & Bottom 5

1. Empathy
2. Developer
3. Restorative
4. Responsibility
5. Harmony
6. Connectedness

_____

30. Command
31. Ideation
32. Futuristic
33. Significance
34. Achiever

Jimmy's Top 6 & Bottom 5

1. Achiever
2. Self-Assurance
3. Command
4. Relator
5. Learner
6. Responsibility

_____

30. Input
31. Developer
32. Includer
33. Context
34. Empathy

When Jimmy and I first started talking about writing this book together, I had no idea his and Karen's strengths would make for such an amazing contrast. I have to say, in all the years

I have been coaching and the thousands of people I've helped with this tool, I have never seen two people who are more opposite! And it's not just that three of Jimmy's bottom-five strengths are in Karen's top five; to make matters worse, two of his top five are in Karen's bottom five. This is so opposite that if this couple came to me for premarital counseling, I might swallow hard at the idea of them getting married.

What stands out to me right away is how opposite—not just different—these two people are. From her strengths I can see that Karen is empathetic; she loves people and feels a personal, inherent desire to see people overcome what has damaged them and grow into all they can be. She likes for people to get along and has an instinctive ability to keep the peace and build teams. For her nothing happens by coincidence; everything happens for a reason, and she feels the pain or celebration of almost everyone she meets. When life is filled with these kinds of opportunities and activities, Karen is most content.

Jimmy, on the other hand, is the least inspired by 60 percent of the things Karen finds most inspiring. His Empathy® ranking is at thirty-four, whereas Karen's is at number one—meaning he feels none of the emotional sensitivity Karen feels. For Karen, being empathetic actually produces that brain-energizing endorphin that makes her feel fantastic. In similar situations, however, Jimmy does not feel that rewarding endorphin and more than likely feels a little drained by lengthy, emotionally taxing moments.

Karen's Developer® ranking is at number two, and she feels strongly motivated to help people. She also wants to see systems improve incrementally and has patience when she sees progress emerging. By contrast, Jimmy's Developer® is number thirty-one, so he gets very little endorphin reward from seeing people incrementally come along. Jimmy's Context® is number thirty-three, meaning he doesn't really care for what happened yesterday. He is much more interested in tomorrow. The problem is, Karen has no interest in tomorrow because her Futuristic® is number thirty-two; and because her Restorative® strength is number three, she is actually much more interested in fixing things that have not worked in the past. In order to do that, she has to know about its history—which is the opposite of tomorrow.

Jimmy loves to get things done and is highly motivated to action, so Achiever® is his number one. Karen has Achiever® at the most extreme opposite—number thirty-four. To her, achievement provides nothing like the reward that it does for Jimmy. Jimmy loves to bring structure to complex problems and feels strongest when making decisions. He has great presence and feels most comfortable leading, so his Command® strength is his number three. Karen, on the other hand, has Command® at number thirty. She isn't interested in making complex decisions and has no desire to lead big teams. It doesn't do anything for her to face complex organizations, and it certainly doesn't give her an endorphin rush to be in charge.

Jimmy loves to learn and has Learner® at number five. He is fascinated by learning, and loves new ideas. But Karen has Ideation® at number thirty-one, meaning she isn't interested in new ideas very much. She probably doesn't really want to hear about Jimmy's new ideas as often as he would like to talk about them.

From the opposite way these two are wired, you can see how easy it was for them to disagree. Imagine how hard it must have been to feel the way they did—to have such natural and genuine tendencies that are so opposite one another. It would be easy to recognize their differences and decide that it is too hard to make it work. Earlier Jimmy said: "I would see something in Karen that was different from me, and I didn't understand. I would reject her and verbally lash out at her. She would get hurt and retaliate both to defend herself and to correct me."

If they both had known their Clifton StrengthsFinder® results and used the strengths language to identify and call out what was right in each other, how different would their early years have been?

I think if Karen had learned sooner that Jimmy's Empathy® strength was number thirty-four, and if Jimmy had known it was Karen's number one, their patience for each other in this particular regard would have been much higher. She would have recognized that he does not willfully withhold Empathy®, and he would have understood that she can't help becoming emotionally invested in the people she meets. Understanding would have made much of the pain go away, because they would have sooner understood how the other was wired. Being wired in a certain way is different from being difficult on purpose.

> IT CHANGES EVERYTHING ABOUT THE WAY YOU RELATE WHEN YOU REALIZE YOUR SPOUSE IS NOT TRYING TO HURT YOU. YOUR SPOUSE LITERALLY JUST DOESN'T HAVE THE TOOLS TO SEE WHAT YOU SEE, AND HE OR SHE WILL LIKELY NEVER BE AS GOOD AT IT AS YOU ARE.

FOUR TYPES OF STRENGTHS

There are four different ways that your strengths can show themselves to the world:

1. UNDERUSED STRENGTH

When people are unaware that they have a strength, they do not see the connection between their endorphin reward and their talent. They don't understand why they act the way they do. As a result, their talent could be really effective and powerful, but it is underutilized. Consequently neither they nor the people around them see or enjoy the benefit of their strength because it is simply underused. At this point, Gallup® would call it a *talent* because it is loaded with potential but has no purposeful expression. It has not yet become a strength.

2. HEALTHY STRENGTH

Strengths are healthy when they are understood and purposefully used in a balanced way for the benefit of the users and the people around them. A talent becomes a strength when skill, experience, or knowledge is applied to the talent. In this expression, the person usually shows healthy levels of self-awareness and has applied effort to grow the talent into true strength. It is a win for that person and for everyone around him or her.

3. OVERUSED STRENGTH

Here again, low self-awareness is often the culprit. People have talents and so love the endorphin rush they get from exercising the talents that they are willing to practice them even if it hurts others. In this situation, the offering is so *loud* that it's bothersome to the people around them. People keep the offenders at arm's length and make faces that say, "What you are doing is too loud. Please turn it down or go away." The talented people often interpret this kind of response as complete rejection, when in fact, all that is being corrected is those particular strengths' over-expression. Don't be too loud.

4. TALENT/STRENGTH COUNTERFEIT

Just as a shadow reveals that something real is nearby, the counterfeit reveals that a real strength is nearby. The challenges are knowing when you are confronting a counterfeit and not making the most of your strength. Buying into the counterfeit will damage you and those around you. For example, If Karen had bought into the counterfeit—the false label—that says she is just a bleeding heart or an emotional wreck, then she eventually would have downplayed an entire part of herself: her empathetic nature. In doing so, she would have neutralized a powerful, God-given talent: Empathy®.

Strengths Based Marriage Challenge

1. Identify the strengths you have in common. If you have any, talk specifically about how you use that shared strength in your lives.
2. Look for strengths that might point you and your spouse in opposite directions and talk about how that plays out in your marriage.

3. Do your differences cause misunderstandings? How?
4. Talk about where your strengths based joy is, especially in the behaviors that seem so opposite, so that you can see where the good in each strength lies.

FOUR

THE POWER OF CHANGE

Jimmy Evans, Marriage Expert

O ver the years the primary complaint I have heard from married people is they want to improve their marriages but their spouses are unwilling. Typically they have pleaded with their spouses to change and get help, but there has been little or no action. So they are in pain and don't know what to do.

After thirty years as a marriage counselor, I have learned that spouses in that condition aren't helpless victims. In fact, there is a lot they can do to change their marriages even if their spouses don't do anything. It is simply a matter of thinking, speaking, and acting in the right manner and with the right attitude.

I don't want to imply there is a secret formula that magically changes everything in a marriage. It requires hard work, change, and dedication, and the results are not guaranteed. I have seen dramatic results in a large number of marriages, however, when one spouse is willing to do the right thing first and then trust that the marriage can be changed.

For this to happen, first it is necessary to understand that the only thing you can change is yourself. And when you change, your marriage changes. To begin the process of change, you will have to lose the "My spouse is the problem, and when he or she changes everything will be good" mentality if you have it.

I don't doubt that your spouse has issues. But did you realize that you marry to your level of emotional health? We almost always marry a person who matches us. It is true of our strengths, but it is also true of our weaknesses.

As an example, dominant people almost always marry a person who is compliant. A dominant man will find a sweet, compliant woman who accommodates his strong personality and lets him control things. A dominant woman will find a sensitive, nice guy who accommodates her strong personality and allows her to be in control.

In marriage, health marries health and unhealthly marries unhealthly. I have a naturally strong personality, and as a young man I was never attracted to a strong woman, regardless of her appearance. I was attracted to quiet, sweet girls who accommodated my dominant personality.

My wife, Karen, had very low self-esteem when we met. She was beautiful, sweet, and allowed me to be in control. So we were the perfect match! Well, not really. Even though we matched emotionally, we were both very unhealthy. You see, even though we marry to our level of emotional health, dominance never works in marriage. Marriage is about sharing and treating each other as equals. No one should ever dominate the relationship or put his or her spouse down in any way. Healthy people don't desire to dominate others or put them down, nor do they want to be dominated or demeaned.

But, for some reason, unhealthy people do. And when they do, the satisfaction of the marriage craters. The person dominating the relationship loses respect for the spouse he or she controls and puts down. And the person being dominated loses respect for the spouse who is disrespecting and controlling him or her. What that person thought was the perfect match ends up being very painful and frustrating.

And the interesting thing is, both spouses believe that if the other person would change, the marriage would be fixed. Learning how to understand your strengths and those of your spouse will be incredibly helpful in improving your marriage. But it is also true of learning your weaknesses—and all of us have weaknesses.

I told you in the previous chapter that my wife and I were on the verge of divorce early in our marriage. I was a male chauvinist pig who was very dominant. What changed me was my wife's changing and becoming emotionally healthy. Early in our marriage, we were both a mess. We both acted in immature and unhealthy ways and pushed each other's buttons until things blew up.

But then my wife began to change. She stopped allowing me to say and do the things I did before. She wasn't mean about it. She gained confidence and began standing up for herself in a mature and gracious manner. She also began to treat me a lot better than I deserved. That really got my attention.

Ultimately it broke through my hard heart and convicted me of the wrong ways I talked to her and treated her. And so, as she stood up to me and yet loved me in a gracious manner, our marriage changed . . . because she was changing. It's just like being on a teeter-totter: when the person on the other side makes a movement, it directly affects you. The same is true in marriage. When you change, your marriage changes.

You are not a victim, and your spouse is not all of the problem or solution. Focus on yourself and not your spouse. Ask yourself some tough questions and answer them. It might also be a good idea to ask others you trust to give you some input. Here are some questions to ask yourself:

- *What would it be like to be married to me?*
- *What are my worst traits, and what can I do to change them?*
- *How emotionally healthy am I? And how does that affect my marriage?*
- *Am I generous in meeting my spouse's needs? Do I only think about myself? Do I only meet the needs in my spouse that I share or agree with?*
- *What does my spouse really love that I am not doing?*
- *Am I treating my spouse the way I want to be treated or how I believe my spouse deserves to be treated?*

Let me conclude my part in this chapter by describing an interesting but disturbing dynamic in marriage. In marriage counseling over the years, I have witnessed a very bizarre thing that shocked me before I understood it.

It would always begin with a husband or wife complaining to me that his or her spouse was the problem and wouldn't change.

Next, I would ask the complaining party to invite his or her spouse to visit with me alone. If that happened, I would work with the spouse to engage the process of improving the marriage and being willing to change. If the person agreed, we would begin. As that spouse engaged in counseling and began to change for the better, a surprising thing often happened. The spouse who came to me in the first place would leave the marriage.

Surprised? I was! And do you know why the complaining spouse left the marriage? It was because when the husband or wife changed, it exposed the other spouse's flaws. They could no longer claim the other spouse was the entire problem. In order to make the marriage work, the complaining spouse would have to start dealing with his or her own issues. And some wouldn't. That spouse had lived so long in the prideful deception that he or she was fine but the other spouse was messed up. The complaining spouse refused to humble himself or herself and face the reality of his or her own problems.

Once I understood this dynamic, I had a different response to spouses coming to me alone for help. I made sure they understood their spouses were not the entire problem. And I also made sure they were willing to deal with their own issues first. From that point forward, I never had a husband or wife leave after his or her spouse changed.

You have the power to change yourself, and that will be the key to changing your marriage. It is better when both spouses are willing to do it. But even if your spouse isn't willing, you are not a victim and you are not powerless. Focus on yourself and become the spouse you need to be. As you change, your marriage will change.

Allan Kelsey, Strengths Expert

These are insightful words from Jimmy about change and personal responsibility. So how do you change your thinking and sense of personal responsibility toward your marriage when your experience has left you deflated? I have found that taking a strengths approach to *your* life first—and then to your spouse's—is a tangible way to walk down that road.

My experience of coaching people in relationships has shown me that opposites attract in marriage (just as Jimmy's marriage shows, and mine too); but by contrast, I have often found that sameness attracts in remarriage. People justify this by saying that their first marriages were "opposites attract" kinds of things, and since that didn't work, they have swung to the other side of the spectrum. This time they've chosen spouses who are much more like them, thinking sameness will fix the problem. Unfortunately, the real problem is revealed by that old proverb: *Wherever you go, there you are.*

In Jimmy's case, he and Karen could not be more opposite. On paper they easily could have gone their separate ways by now, but as he pointed out, it was Karen's action of personal responsibility in the marriage that really began to heal things for them. A marriage that begins with either differences or similarities can really benefit from someone's taking personal

> **STRENGTHENING YOUR MARRIAGE IS LESS ABOUT FINDING SOMEONE WHO IS AN IDEAL FIT AND MORE ABOUT PERSONALLY OWNING YOUR PART.**

responsibility. The most tangible way to do that is by using your strengths.

Taking a strengths approach to your life and your spouse's not only calls out the best in your spouse but also provides access to the natural endorphins that reward you when you use your strengths. This is important because though your spouse may not reward you initially for an action of kindness or generosity, your endorphins will. And let's face it: we all need a little encouragement to keep going if results are slow in the beginning.

How do you take personal responsibility for your part in the marriage using your strengths? The answer has three parts:

1. Understand yourself.
2. Understand your spouse.
3. Change your thinking.

It starts with your getting to know who you are from a strengths perspective. First, read your Clifton StrengthsFinder® results and get to know what those top-five strengths really mean for you. Human development psychologists agree that much of our growth as people hinges on self-awareness. If you don't know who you are, then your responses to things are unpredictable to others, and worst of all, to you too. Take your strengths results to your spouse or your friends and show them your paragraph descriptions. Ask them to tell you what they see in you, using the description as a starting point. The more you hear from others about how you use that strength, the more your confidence will build. The revelation that you truly have remarkable ability, and that others see it in you, will become a powerful part of your reality.

Next, take some time to get familiar with your spouse's strengths. It's common knowledge that our favorite subject is ourselves, so take your spouse's results and go through the descriptions together. This activity will provide content for a date-night discussion, and it will deepen your understanding of each other. When appropriate, have your friends tell you about how they see your spouse's strengths in action. It will deepen your insight about your spouse. Also, in your conversation with friends, be sure to ask about where they see the joy in an action or behavior that displays the strength in your spouse. Recognizing the joy in your spouse's strengths will give you meaningful insight into what actions provide rewards for your spouse.

Finally, change your thinking. Look at the regular behavior of your spouse through a strengths lens. Can you see your spouse's strengths in play? Here's an example: as an Achiever®, I love to get stuff done; so when my wife, Stephanie, sees me getting things done around the house, she can assign that behavior to my Achiever® and recognize the satisfaction of completion as my reward. If you can see your spouse's actions through a strengths lens, then you can better understand your spouse's motivations and recognize the corresponding rewards of his or her actions.

Let me conclude this chapter with a story that illustrates this idea. Earlier in our marriage, Stephanie and I lived in Houston, Texas, and I worked in a very sweaty outdoor environment every day. One Thursday evening in early fall, I got home a little later than normal because my clients had been particularly fussy that day. We had planned for friends to come over for dinner the next night (Friday), and as I pulled into the driveway, I noticed the yard needed to be mowed pretty badly. I also knew, based on my typical

Friday, that I would probably not get home in time to mow the lawn before our guests arrived. (Can you see my Strategic® strength in play here too?) Since I was already sweaty, I decided that now was as good a time as any to mow the lawn. So I parked the car, ran into the garage, got the mower out, and started mowing.

Stephanie was inside and had been keeping my dinner warm. She knew I was running a little late (thank you, mobile phones!) and was ready to see me. It surprised her when she heard the mower running outside. To make matters worse, the sun was going down. Well, as an Achiever®, I feel a lot of joy in completing action, so there was no way I was going to stop mowing just because the silly sun had gone down. I could still see—*kind of.* I pushed on and got the yard mowed, finishing by moonlight and flashlight. (All of you Achievers®, you understand what I'm talking about.)

When I got inside, the look on Stephanie's face said it all. I knew I was in trouble, but I was perplexed. Couldn't she see that I had mowed the yard nicely for tomorrow night's guests? I was not ready for what she said next: "I wish I was grass! At least then I would get mowed every week." She was clearly unhappy.

I didn't know what to say. I was tired and sweaty and had just finished a long day by doing something I thought would be a good thing. How had this ended so badly? I had felt blessing in my heart when I mowed, so why were we fighting now that it was done?

What Stephanie read from my actions was that the grass had priority over her. She was frustrated that I hadn't come in to greet her. She wanted me to tell her about my plan to mow, to make her a part of the decision. And she wanted me to value her and the effort she had put into the meal that was waiting for me. In short, she missed me and was looking forward to connecting when I finally got home. Instead, she felt as if she were waiting in line behind a lawn mower and the grass.

Both Stephanie and I had good intentions in our hearts toward each other; and, truth be told, we both had been eager to see each other that Thursday evening. There was no latent anger or animosity hanging in the air. We talked it out and worked through our different interpretations of the events of that night. Using our strengths language gave us the words we needed to articulate accurately our real motives and emotions. In the end, we knew we were on the same team and wanted the best for each other on that day and the next.

But I don't know how we would have dug out of that hole without the language of strengths to point to real motivation and to adequately express what was going on in our hearts.

Strengths Based Marriage Challenge

1. Consider revisiting an old disagreement that you have already resolved and try unpacking it using a strengths perspective.
2. Using the same example, look for the power in the contribution, look for the misunderstanding, and explain your motivations in the moment.
3. Explain how you would like that action to be interpreted in the future—especially if it was misunderstood.

4. Consider what it would mean to your marriage to change your mind-set. How can you consider the strength in play behind your spouse's every action? And how can you adjust the way you interpret that action through a strengths lens?

FIVE

PROMISES OF PAIN

Jimmy Evans, Marriage Expert

He was just about the worst husband I had ever met. A friend of mine asked me to help him because he was having marriage problems. After a few minutes of talking, he informed me that his wife lived in an apartment downtown and he lived in a house.

"So, you are separated?" I asked.

He replied, "No, she has never been in the house."

Shocked, I questioned why.

He said, "I don't want her in the house. That is why I rented her an apartment downtown."

I then asked, "You mean you have never lived together?"

He replied, "No, and we never will. And that is one of the reasons we are having problems. She just can't accept it."

After a few minutes of talking to him, I realized he controlled every aspect of their relationship. In fact, he told me he had never had a satisfactory relationship with a woman and didn't trust them. Having done a lot of counseling, I knew there was something deeper going on than a disagreement about living in separate places. My suspicions were soon confirmed after I said this to him: "Tell me about your father and mother's relationship."

In emotional and graphic terms he told me that his mother was a dominating witch who had emasculated his father every day of his life. He told me that he had promised himself that it would never happen to him. And of course it didn't—but he was every woman's worst nightmare and his mother's soul twin, and he didn't even realize it.

In promising himself he would never be dominated by a woman, he was making an inner vow. Inner vows can be very dangerous and cause untold pain in our lives and the lives around us. And almost every person has made them. We make inner vows to comfort ourselves. We don't do it because we are evil or want to cause pain.

In response to relational problems, abuse, rejection, poverty, failure, loss, or some other painful issue, we say things like this to ourselves:

- *I'll never be poor again.*
- *No man or woman will ever treat me like that.*
- *I'll never make my children work like this.*
- *I'll never make my kids go to church every time the doors are opened.*
- *I'll never let anyone hurt me again.*
- *I'll never work all the time like my parents.*
- *I'll never be vulnerable again.*

Even though some inner vows can be pretty harmless, others can cause long-lasting pain. In this situation the man who wouldn't let his wife into the house dominated everything about their relationship; his inner vow became a promise of pain for himself and all the women in his life.

One of the most dangerous dynamics of inner vows is that within any area you have an inner vow operating, you are typically unteachable and irrational. While I talked to the husband who wouldn't let his wife live with him, he had a smirk on his face during the entire conversation. I told him he was wrong to control his wife and to insist she live in an apartment. Even though I'm sure you agree with me, he mocked me and thought he was a relational genius.

In fact, when I told him that the promise he had made to himself—that no woman would dominate him—was at the core of his thoughts, motivation, and behavior, he said, "Yeah, I understand all that, but that has nothing to do with it." Oh, yes, it did.

When I was growing up I didn't live in poverty, but I lived pretty close. One of the most embarrassing things about not having money was that I didn't have many clothes. I went through middle school and high school with a couple of shirts, one pair of jeans, and one pair of shoes. Many of my friends had money, and they had nice clothes and plenty of them.

In response to the shame I experienced, I said to myself one day, "When I grow up I'm going to have nice clothes." Fast-forward twenty years, and Karen and I are in a big argument about my spending too much money on clothes. In fact, I had bought so many clothes I couldn't get them in my closet without getting rid of something.

Karen said, "Jimmy, you are a clotheshorse. You buy way too many clothes."

I replied, "I don't buy too many clothes. Our closets are just too small."

Remember what I said about inner vows making you unteachable and irrational? That was me!

When I first heard about inner vows and how they can lock us into cycles of pain, I realized I had made many of them growing up. One by one, I began to renounce them and break them. I also told Karen what I was doing and asked her to provide input and keep me accountable.

I know you've been through hard times before and experienced pain in your past. All of us have. Did you make inner vows? Are there areas of your life where you are unteachable and irrational because of the promises you made yourself?

Is there something your spouse and others try to talk to you about, but you are defensive and won't receive input? Inner vows are promises of pain for your future. They can even transmit pain for generations. The solution is to acknowledge them, renounce them, and become accountable to change.

It is healing for your marriage when you humbly acknowledge to your spouse that you have been influenced by an inner vow and are breaking it. Because you know you have been unteachable, irrational, and unapproachable in that area, you are asking for accountability and input. Whereas in the past you have snarled at those who tried to approach you, you now can welcome them and not punish them for being honest.

You will find that your life and marriage are much better without inner vows. Renouncing them puts the past in the past where it belongs, and it allows you to walk into the future without carrying pain with you.

Allan Kelsey, Strengths Expert

There are two primary reasons for knowing and operating in your strengths. First, the strongest contributions of your life will likely come from using your strengths. Second, exercising your strengths results in joy. There is a repeatable reward of endorphin payback we feel when we use our strengths. The thing about this reward, though, is that it cannot discern good from bad. The endorphin rush comes from using your strengths, but your strengths are not inherently good or bad. You use your character and your conscience to make those choices.

Strategic® is number two on my strengths list. I love to use my Strategic® strength to build plans for advancement, to grow organizations, and to help people become their most creative and productive selves. It helps me "begin with the end in mind," as Stephen Covey used to say.[1] I see the end from the beginning, and then it is easy for me to back up and plan toward the objective. This ability can be very helpful to other people, but I could also use my Strategic® nature to plan illegal activities. For example, I could strategize how to evade the police when robbing homes. Now, let's be clear, I would never do such a thing—but I could use my Strategic® strength to plan every possible escape route. That activity would provoke the endorphins in me, providing the chemically induced rush that comes from using my strengths—even though such actions are illegal.

So, what if you made an inner vow to do or be something, and as it turns out, that vow is actually tapping into a strength that you have? In that case, fulfilling your inner vow would produce an endorphin rush; and since those chemicals make a person

> **THE CURIOUS THING ABOUT THIS CHEMICAL FEEL-GOOD EXPERIENCE IS THAT IT RESPONDS ANYTIME A STRENGTH IS BEING USED—NOT JUST WHEN IT IS BEING USED FOR GOOD.**

feel good, it would be easy to connect your inner vow with feeling good! Do you see how sneaky that is?

Take a moment to consider, as Jimmy suggested, any vows that you may have made. They usually sound extreme when said in conversation, like:

I will never . . .
I absolutely hate . . .
That will never happen to me again . . .

Now pause to think about how your strengths may be reinforcing that vow. Consider asking your spouse to help you think through this exercise, because two perspectives here will be clearer than one.

Is it possible that you are inadvertently using a strength to support an inner vow that is actually hurtful to you or destructive to your marriage? Only your patient and transparent honesty will reveal if an inner vow is active in your marriage.

If together you find none in your marriage or individual lives, then do the happy dance and move on. This is not a hurdle you have to jump. On the other hand, if you find an inner vow in your life or in your marriage that is also linked to a strength, then the solution is similar to Jimmy's: acknowledge the vow, identify the strength that is associated with it, renounce the vow, and begin to redirect the strength toward fruitfulness and away from destructive action that could be hurtful to your marriage.

I once worked with a guy we will call Peter. Peter had Positivity® in his top five. He thought things were fine, but Peter's wife was frustrated with him because she felt he didn't really help discipline and direct the kids. Often when there was an issue in the house, Peter would disappear. If confronted, he would downplay the offense and say, "After all, they are just kids." Peter's default position was to lean on the positive side of things. Under normal circumstances, Peter's Positivity® would be balanced by his other strengths—by healthy parenting and by the normal sense of boundaries we all need—but Peter had no such constraints. His Positivity® seemed endless, and it was driving his wife crazy.

After talking with Peter I realized he had made a vow concerning his parenting that was being fed by his strength of Positivity®. You see, Peter had been raised in a home where his dad very seldom gave any praise, and when he did, it usually came with a slant or a manipulation. It was so devastating to Peter that he decided if he ever became a dad, he would always give his kids praise, encouragement, and support.

Without realizing it, Peter had made a vow to *always* be positive with his kids. Because he has the strength of Positivity®, it actually felt good to do the very thing he had vowed to do. The only problem was, it had gone too far and was now negatively affecting the kids and his marriage. "The kids are unruly and he refuses to see it. He sticks his head in the sand and won't deal with anything hard or emotionally charged," his wife said to me.

After helping Peter see the vow that he had made and

understand the strong feelings he gets when he holds a positive perspective about his kids, we were able to separate the vow from his strength of Positivity®. These days Peter is much better. There are days he still lets the kids get a bit too rowdy, but he is much more attentive and no longer afraid to engage with them if needed. His Positivity® is still unshaken and he is one of the most encouraging people you could meet, but he is no longer blind to the real challenges around him. And his wife is much happier.

Strengths Based Marriage Challenge

1. Have you made any inner vows? If so, can you name them? Sometimes we can't see ourselves clearly, so invite your spouse to kindly offer some insight too.
2. If you have identified an inner vow, can you see it being amplified by a strength? What strength(s) are involved?
3. What does the inner vow compel you to do or say? How is that vow made stronger by the strength?
4. How can your spouse help you overcome the inner vow?

SIX

CUTTING THE CORD OF PAIN

Jimmy Evans, Marriage Expert

A n attractive couple was headed toward the altar. I was their premarital counselor, and it was my job to prepare them properly. I really liked them as a couple. She had a very sweet personality and he was a witty, athletic type.

One day during a premarital session, she remarked that he had anger issues. He immediately cocked his head around and gave her a look when she said it. Interested, I asked her to elaborate. She told me that he had never taken his anger out on her in a hurtful way, but he usually focused his anger on himself.

As an example, she told me that when he got angry, he went into the garage and beat himself with wrenches. Surprised, I asked him if it was true.

"Yeah, I do that," he responded.

She continued by saying that he put people in the hospital playing football and enjoyed it. He also drove his car at high speeds and jerked the wheel around as if to tempt fate and vent his anger. That, she said, scared her worse than anything.

After she finished, he acknowledged everything she said.

So I asked him, "Who are you mad at? What is behind all this anger?"

He replied, "I'm not mad at anyone."

I didn't buy it. When someone is that angry, there is a fire burning inside. And in his case it was a bonfire.

Refusing to believe he wasn't mad at anyone, I started down a list of people he could be angry toward. I asked him, "Are you angry at your boss?"

"No," he replied.

"Are you angry at a friend?"

"No."

"Your mother?"

"No, I love my mother," he replied.

"How about your father?" I asked.

He then said: "Well, I don't know the [expletive], but if I ever find him I will kill him."

Bingo!

He went on to tell me that his father had left his mother when she was pregnant with him, and he would never forgive him. He grew up obsessed with the fact he was fatherless, and how wrong it was for his father to have deserted his mother. The anger in him was a direct result of his unforgiveness toward his father. But regardless of whom he was mad at, the people closest to him felt the fallout.

That is always true. It doesn't matter how far behind us our offenders may be; the people in our present receive the punishment—especially our spouses. You could be bitter and unforgiving toward someone who is dead, but those closest to you will pay the price for it.

Back to the story of the young man who was mad at his father. In my office on the day I found out about it, I led him through the process of forgiving his father. At first he was reluctant and said he didn't know if he could do it. I explained that his anger was like an invisible umbilical cord that connected him to his father and the pain of his past.

I also explained that if he didn't forgive his father, his anger would destroy his marriage, his health, and everything important in his life. When I finished explaining all the ramifications of his bitterness, he stared at me for a minute without saying anything. Then he started crying and couldn't stop. He cried for one solid hour, and at the end of it, he looked up at me and said, "Okay, I'm ready to forgive him." And he did. I led him in a prayer to forgive his dad and to entrust any vengeance to the Lord. He forgave his father and put the issue in the past.

The next time the couple came back to my office, the young woman spoke first and said, "He is a different person. Before, we all had to tiptoe around him, trying not to make him mad. Now we can't make him mad. He has totally changed." And he really had. He was a completely different person than before, and without the anger he was ready to be a loving husband.

Forgiveness isn't just something we do once to put the past behind us. It is something we must do every day—especially for those closest to us, such as our spouses. If we don't forgive, we hold grudges and keep points. Before long we grow bitter.

Bitterness is a justice spirit that won't go forward until it receives the satisfaction it desires.

The more bitter we become, the more hard-hearted we become to our spouses and others. We grow more cynical and cold, sarcastic and mean-spirited. And we fall out of love and wonder why we ever got married in the first place.

One of the most important disciplines in marriage is to never go to bed angry—ever. Not at our spouse or anyone else. Even if others are unwilling to say they are sorry or work things out, we can forgive them. It is a critical discipline to keep us emotionally healthy and to keep our hearts tender toward each other.

Here are some sayings I like concerning forgiveness:

- Forgiveness doesn't make the other person right—it just makes me free.
- The inability to forgive is like drinking poison and expecting someone else to die.
- Unforgiveness damages the vessel that stores it worse than anyone you can spit it on.
- Forgiveness is the most self-loving thing we can do.

Is there anyone in your past or your present life you haven't forgiven?

Are you holding something against your spouse?

Do yourself a favor and forgive. Put your grievances in God's hands and trust Him to handle them. He will, and you can be free to live and love.

Allan Kelsey, Strengths Expert

I have heard intimacy therapist Nancy Houston say, "No action has the power to hurt you until you attribute meaning to it." For me, this was a powerful revelation. I deeply understood what she meant.

I grew up in a home where I was told: "Engage the brain before engaging the mouth," and, "Consider what you are about to say and how it will affect others *before* you say it." Over the years I have come to both love and hate those values instilled in my life. I love them because they have taught me to have an "others first" mind-set. But they also left me overly concerned about what others think of me.

This obsession with what others think or feel about me—multiplied by decades of reinforcement—turned me into a connoisseur of interpreted feelings. I believed I was expert in knowing and responding to your feelings before you even had them, because I had been trained to imagine what outcome my words would have. Fast-forward that approach to life and relationships and my marriage to Stephanie, and it created problems.

One of Stephanie's top-five strengths is Belief®, which means she has morals and ethics based values that are really non-negotiable. She often places family first, is steady as the day is long, and sometimes attracts people in turmoil because of her lighthouse-like stability. I love her.

Early on in our marriage, Stephanie and I were introduced to the Clifton StrengthsFinder® assessment. Although its initial input was revelatory, we didn't have any awareness of talent counterfeits, so we had no language to describe the other side of our strengths. The counterfeit for Belief® often appears when people suggest that you see everything in black-and-white, or they call you stubborn or pigheaded. Or it's unearthed when they say things like: "Why can't you acknowledge that life is lived in the gray?" or "Why does everything have to be your way?" Now, this is not how Stephanie lives her life, but people can interpret her this way.

I observed some of these counterfeits in Stephanie's life, and because Belief® was strong in her, those counterfeits came out strong too. The problem was, we didn't know they were counterfeits; I just assumed it was all part of her strength and needed to be embraced. Here is where the pain in our marriage appeared.

My upbringing had taught me to measure people's emotions and to adjust my actions and speech according to my measurement of those emotions. When Stephanie's emotions appeared stubborn to me, I felt conflicted. On one hand I wanted to challenge her emotions, and on the other hand I wanted to back down and make room for her and not offend her. Challenging her or opposing her didn't seem considerate of her emotions, so (many times) I opted to accommodate her. As a result, our marriage began to lean toward imbalance. I began to feel unseen, even though I was the one deferring; and eventually out of sheer frustration, I began to keep score.

It had a devastating impact in our marriage.

> I DIDN'T KNOW WHAT ELSE TO DO, AND I DIDN'T KNOW THAT I WAS MAKING DECISIONS ABOUT HER BASED ON A COUNTERFEIT.

When we first met, Stephanie was drawn to my confidence and decisiveness, while this spineless, deferring version of me was not attractive to her at all. I began keeping score of the times I had deferred to "her way," but since "her way" was actually the counterfeit in play, I was keeping score of a lie. As a result she felt misunderstood. When we spoke, we didn't have the language to accurately describe what was really going on, so we never really resolved the problem. It was hurtful to Stephanie and to me. My only option seemed to be trying to forgive and to tolerate what I didn't understand.

Once we knew about the counterfeits of our strengths, however, we could both talk more accurately about what was going on in our marriage. I then had useful language that allowed me to refer to her strengths in an inviting and supportive way, because I believe the best of who she is will emerge from her strengths. Additionally, being able to accurately identify and discuss counterfeits helped me talk about her actions without resorting to what I believed about her motivations.

In turn, Stephanie helped me see her Belief® strength more clearly, which helped me understand what was really going on in her heart. It clarified her intentions and removed the counterfeit effect.

This conversation made my understanding of her so much deeper. It moved the actions I had attributed to her Belief® strength out of a frustrating category into a different category— one of counterfeits. This counterfeit category may be factual, but it lied about her motivations. The more we discussed counterfeits with useful strengths based vocabulary, the more effectively I understood her real heart and the truth about her motivations.

Furthermore, Stephanie began to make intentional and subtle adjustments to her behavior to help realign the way people interpreted her actions. She wanted her actions to appear more consistent with her real motivations, her real strengths. It was an immediate blessing to our marriage and it deepened our love for each other.

Strengths Based Marriage Challenge

1. Identify your strengths and the strengths of your spouse.
2. Discuss the counterfeits to each strength. Pay close attention to the difference between how you feel when you are acting from your strength and how your strength is interpreted by your spouse or others. That is where the counterfeit lives.
3. Undo the power of the counterfeit by opening your heart and explaining the real motivation behind the action for each of your strengths. Transparency is the antidote to a counterfeit.
4. It may feel a little odd, but help your spouse understand how to interpret your actions when you are using your strength. It will reveal your heart.

SEVEN

THE HEALING JOURNEY OF MARRIAGE

Jimmy Evans, Marriage Expert

There are many theories about why we select the mates we do. Biologists insist we base our choices on genetic traits. Sociologists claim we base them on status and social parity. But there is another quite interesting theory. It states that we select our mates based on the traits they possess that match the positive and negative effects of our parents or caretakers early in life.

In their book *Getting the Love You Want*, Dr. Harville Hendrix and Dr. Helen LaKelly Hunt explain their thesis on the origins of romantic love and why we select and marry our spouses. According to their theory, we select our mates because they have the best ability to heal us from the wounds of our past. The positive traits they possess match the unmet needs from our past, while their negative traits match the unfinished business we had with parents who wounded us. And so, according to their theory, whether we realize it or not, we marry someone with the hopes of being healed.[1]

Before reading their book, I had taught the same basic

truth in seminars for years. I don't have the academic or clinical background of Dr. Hendrix or Dr. Hunt. But I have made the observation time and again that we are attracted to our mates for a reason, and when done correctly, marriage is a healing journey. I believe that God has invested within us inherent traits that match the needs of our spouses. If we use these traits to serve and love our spouses, it not only meets their needs, but it also heals them from the wounds of their past.

After forty-three years of marriage and having counseled thousands of couples, it has become very clear that we can look to the Bible to understand the basic needs of men and women.

As an example, aside from the basic need for love, the number one need of men is respect. This can be seen in Ephesians 5:22–24, where it says, "Wives, be subject to your own husbands, as to the Lord. For the husband is the head of the wife, as Christ also is the head of the church, He Himself being the Savior of the body. But as the church is subject to Christ, so also the wives ought to be to their husbands in everything" (NASB). This does not give men the right to dominate but rather empowers women to love their husbands through sacrificial honor. Therefore, the deepest wound a man can experience is disrespect or dishonor. When a wife praises her husband she is not only meeting his primary need as a man, she is also healing the wounds of his past.

Besides love, the primary need of women is security. Ephesians 5 goes on to say in verses 28–30, "So husbands ought also to love their own wives as their own bodies. He who loves his own wife loves himself; for no one ever hated his own flesh, but nourishes and cherishes it, just as Christ also does the church, because we are members of His body."

Little girls and women need to know that they are going to be cared for, nurtured, and protected by a selfless, sacrificial man. When a husband creates an atmosphere of security for his wife, he is meeting her primary need as well as healing any wounds she might have from her past of abandonment, lack of nurturing, abuse, and so on.

The title of this chapter is "The Healing Journey of Marriage." I know that it might be a little shocking and maybe even disturbing for some people to think about marriage in those terms because for many people marriage has damaged them more than any other relationship in life. To think of it in terms of a healing journey is hard to do.

But the reason marriage hurts us is because we do it wrong. I truly believe if we relate to our spouses properly, marriage is a healing journey that gets better over time. And the reason it gets better is because we become more and more healed and more in love with our spouses as our healers.

It is true of Karen and me. We fought so much for the first few years of our marriage that we became numb. We rejected each other's differences, and both of us used wounding words to defend ourselves and punish each other. And we barely survived it.

The change in our marriage took place as Karen began to heal and began acting in a more mature manner. In her case, I wasn't her healer at that point. It was her relationship with God that began the greatest healing in her life. But as she matured and I changed, a new dynamic began in our relationship.

The first thing that happened is that we stopped rejecting and judging each other's differences. We grew in respect and admiration for each other and realized we were different by

God's design. We also began to serve each other by meeting different needs we had previously judged and rejected in each other. I will discuss these needs in a future chapter.

Another thing we did that transformed our relationship is that we gave each other the right to complain without paying a price. In other words, we opened a customer relations counter in our marriage as a place where we could complain in a safe manner. Just as in a good department store where you feel safe to shop, there is a customer relations counter in our marriage with a friendly person behind it to deal with problems you might have.

Most marriages don't have a customer relations counter. In fact, one of the hallmarks of hurting marriages is defensiveness. One or both spouses have trained the other not to bring up certain problems, or World War III will break out. And that is why their marriages can't produce the healing that is possible if they could just talk.

Complaining isn't criticizing. Criticizing focuses on the other and what is wrong with that person. It is damaging. Complaining is simply stating how I am feeling. My feelings may not be right, but they are real—and I just need to talk about them. I need to do so in a manner that doesn't attack or judge my spouse. I am just saying that I need to talk to you about a feeling I am having, and I will give you an opportunity to respond without being attacked.

It is important to learn how to complain without being critical or harsh. We also need to learn to start every confrontation in a positive and loving manner, and to let our spouses know we are committed to the relationship. Threats and harshness doom a conversation to failure before it ever starts.

But the most important thing we do to allow the healing

process to begin is to invite our spouses to open up to us and complain. We need to let them know that we want to please them and be the best spouses we can be. We must prove to them that we are a safe place, and they will not pay a price for being honest—even if we have to work through some negative emotions and tough issues.

This is where the healing journey of marriage begins. As we respect each other's differences, serve each other, and allow open communication in a safe manner, we meet our healer. Out of thirty-four strengths in the Clifton StrengthsFinder® assessment, my thirty-fourth is Empathy®. It is Karen's number-one strength. Talk about marrying your opposite! No, she isn't my opposite—she is my complement. She completes me—and her Empathy® has healed a part of my heart that was damaged long ago.

Because she has been instrumental in my healing, I love her all the more. And now that we are both healed, loving each other is so much easier and more rewarding. We married our spouses for many reasons. But one of the reasons we married them is so they could heal us. That is the way God designed marriage—to be a healing journey.

Allan Kelsey, Strengths Expert

In marriage, we are often drawn to the elements in our spouses that complement our own. They can complement by way of healing or by way of amplifying. Our attraction could be built around differences that are complementary or differences that bring balance. Whatever you saw in each other that brought the two of you together has enough power to *keep* the two of you together, but it is going to take a new strengths based language to do it.

Take Stephanie and me, for example.

You will notice from the diagram, which shows our upper and lower Clifton StrengthsFinder® results, how vastly different Stephanie and I are. The purpose of the diagram is to show how my highest-ranking strengths are among her lowest and how my lowest-ranking strengths are among her highest.

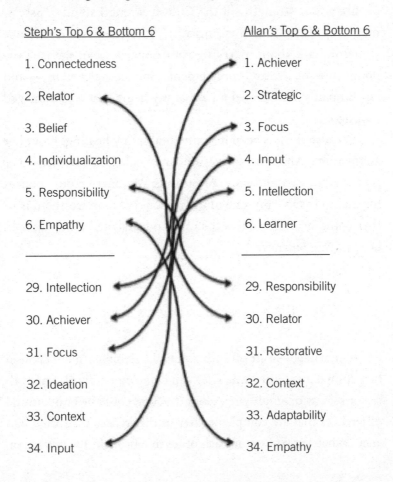

Steph's Top 6 & Bottom 6

1. Connectedness
2. Relator
3. Belief
4. Individualization
5. Responsibility
6. Empathy

29. Intellection
30. Achiever
31. Focus
32. Ideation
33. Context
34. Input

Allan's Top 6 & Bottom 6

1. Achiever
2. Strategic
3. Focus
4. Input
5. Intellection
6. Learner

29. Responsibility
30. Relator
31. Restorative
32. Context
33. Adaptability
34. Empathy

Four out of my top-five strengths are in Stephanie's bottom seven, and three of my bottom strengths are in Stephanie's top eight. My Empathy® is number thirty-four, and it's in Stephanie's top eight. We are drawn to each other for different reasons and certainly have different strengths. They are different enough that we see life quite differently, which can either heal us or drive a wedge between us. If you look at my upper strengths you will notice that they all have to do with action, tasks, and accomplishment. If you look at Stephanie's upper strengths, you will notice that they are mostly people and relationship oriented.

This means that I love to strategize and get things done, while she loves to relate and hang out with people. I am an introvert and recharge through solitude, while she is an extrovert who recharges amid relationship with others. The strategy that drains her fires me up, and the people who recharge her can cause me to yearn for solitude again. Man, talk about opposites, right? No. She is most definitely my complement.

Now let me tell you how she heals me.

Stephanie has Individualization® in her top six strengths. People who have this strength are fascinated by the uniqueness of individuals. They find great interest in the nuanced differences in people and celebrate those differences. When I first met Stephanie, she seemed so interested in me—not only because I had a crazy South African accent, but also because she has Individualization® and she found uniqueness in me. But she didn't just see it and walk away, the way you might if you saw an ostrich at the zoo; she saw *me*, and I knew it. She has a way of interacting with me that makes me feel seen. Have you ever spent time with someone like that? When you hang out with them, they make you feel seen? It's as though they look at you or interact with you in a way that leaves you thinking, *That person really gets me beyond just normal understanding.*

I *love* this about Stephanie. She really sees me and our two daughters. I feel deeply affirmed by her just by spending time with her, and this is her normal way of living. She doesn't feel like she is doing anything special, but to me, it is as life giving as a deep clean breath. I try to tell her, "I love how you see me," but she just shrugs her shoulders and smiles—to her it just feels normal. She complements me in this way.

In our marriage, Stephanie is the one who nurtures relationships. She is the one who stays up late to talk to our daughters and will spend the energy to ensure that the relationships we all have are good. She is great at it, and it actually feels good to her to do it because she feels the endorphins that are released from acting in her strengths. She gets a reward for doing it. We need her and her gift in our family, because that relational power is not going to come from me very effectively. My strengths are best used when we need to build the shelves in my daughters' bedroom or get a savings plan for our daughters' school fund.

In addition, all my strategizing and intellectual strengths can help me find a very informed and sensible way to move forward, but that doesn't always mean that I have all the confidence I need to make it happen. Sometimes I second-guess myself and vacillate over which path to take, or whether I should even take one at all. This is also where Stephanie heals me. She has a Spidey-sense for insecure leadership, and it drives her crazy. You see, her strengths set her up for amazing confidence and bold, unwavering faith for the things she takes on.

When I have the smarts to make an informed decision but waver in my confidence over its outcome, she doesn't know what to do with that wavering. She doesn't have receptors to receive that kind of information; it just makes her crazy. So if I display insecure leadership, she leans in and lends me her unwavering faith. In those seasons I practice with her power, all the while getting stronger myself. I am a better leader because my wife has helped me get there. I can choose to let her uniqueness heal me, and it's beautiful.

To conclude, I want to tell you about a phenomenon I have observed from coaching hundreds of couples using the Clifton StrengthsFinder® assessment. I call it *spousal transference.* Spousal transference is when someone operates stronger in a particular strength than they normally would because it is high on their spouse's top strengths. For example, I typically have low Empathy®, but it is Stephanie's number six, so she is *much* stronger and better at it than I am. Ordinarily my Empathy® is seldom in action, and when it is, it's pretty weak. But I find that the more time I spend with Stephanie, the more effective my Empathy® becomes. I find myself actually being better at it than its number thirty-four position would normally allow. The stronger the strength is in her, or the higher it is on her list, the stronger my ability in that particular area becomes. When I am routinely around her, my Empathy® outplays its position on my list. But when we get separated by travel, for example, my Empathy® falls back down to its normal position again. I lose my superpowers and go back to being normal Allan again.

To my knowledge, this phenomenon has never been scientifically validated, but my repeated observation of this phenomenon in hundreds of couples has made me a believer in spousal transference. Now that Dr. Hendrix and Dr. Hunt have confirmed that we marry the one who is most likely to heal us, I can see how spousal transference is more than just hypothesis. Thank you, Stephanie. I know it sounds cheesy, but in the most scientific way, you complete me!

Strengths Based Marriage Challenge

1. Which strengths in your spouse attract you? Why?
2. Describe a behavior that attracts you to your spouse. Explain how that behavior is a manifestation of one of your spouse's strengths.
3. Do you operate in one of your spouse's strengths more powerfully than its presence on your list should allow? If so, which one? Discuss what that looks like.
4. In what strengths based way does your spouse complete you?

SPEAKING LOVE TO YOUR SPOUSE'S HEART

EIGHT

THE SECRET OF SUCCESSFUL COMMUNICATION

Jimmy Evans, Marriage Expert

One of the greatest challenges in any marriage is communication. And the greatest single challenge in communicating with our spouses is our differences. It would be so much easier to talk if they were just like us—felt like us, thought like us, had our needs, had our personalities, and so forth. But they don't and never will. Never!

At some point, if we are going to grow in our ability to communicate with our spouses, we have to accept without any negative attitude that they are different from us. If we don't completely accept this, then we will continue to be frustrated and to take it out on them through lectures, shame, harsh words, or silence.

One of the surest ways to fail is to try to change something that is unchangeable. Your spouse is different from you. That is unchangeable. Don't waste another ounce of energy trying to change your spouse. The key to success is to understand your spouse. That is what this book is all about.

Here is something I say to couples in my seminars that always gets an interesting response: *If you married someone normal, they aren't like you.* I like to see people's faces when I say that. A lot of them look at me as if I just told them they're weird or something.

But I didn't. I just called their spouses normal. And I told them the truth. If you marry a normal man or woman, they will be very different from you. And to succeed in marriage you must understand and respect those differences.

In the next chapter I will talk about the four major needs of men and women. But in this chapter I want to tell you about the single primary need of both men and women. I call these the *mega-needs* because they are the driving forces of how we see life and how we hear everything that is said to us.

Women have four major needs, but their primary need—their mega-need—is security. We see the evidence of this in Ephesians 5, as discussed earlier. Women need to know they are going to be cared for by a sacrificial, selfless husband who is connected to them emotionally. And because this is a woman's primary need, everything she hears is encrypted through it.

When a husband talks to his wife, he will never succeed in communicating with her if what he says makes her feel less secure. In other words, even though he could be using all the right words, she is listening to more than his words. She is listening to his attitude and the tone of his voice.

She can tell if his heart isn't really connected to hers. She can tell if she isn't really a priority or if he sees her as a burden and a distraction from something else he is more interested in. And if a wife discerns that her husband is distracted or burdened by her, she will not accept his words to the contrary.

For a man to successfully communicate with his wife, he must encrypt every word with security. Regardless of what the conversation is about, she must hear through the tone of his voice and his attitude something like this: *Honey, you come first. You are the most important thing in my life, and you are worth anything else I need to sacrifice. You are not a burden to me. You are the love of my life. Even if I don't get what I want, you will get what you want because I will do anything to make sure you are taken care of.*

When a wife hears security in her husband's words, she relaxes and can hear what is being said. And of course, a husband must follow through with his words to make sure her need for security is met on every level. And let me tell you, from more than forty years of experience, when you sacrifice to meet your wife's need for security, there is a big payoff. It is worth whatever you have to do.

But men are different. We don't have the same need for security. Our mega-need is honor, so we see life through that lens and hear everything through that filter. Regardless of what is being said to a man, if he discerns disrespect in it, he will reject it.

Early in our marriage I told Karen that the way she said something to me was as important to me as what she was saying. That is the common sentiment of men. Even though we may be big and strong on the outside, we are very tender in our egos.

Because of this, a man will naturally gravitate to the place he gets the most respect and avoid places or people that make him feel disrespected. When a wife is communicating with her husband, she must understand this reality. Everything she says to him must be encrypted with honor and respect. Regardless of what she is saying, he must hear in her attitude and the tone of her voice something like this: *Honey, I believe in you. You are a good man and you have what it takes. I am your cheerleader and your biggest fan. We are on the same team and I am committed to you.*

I want you wives to know that you are your husbands' equals in every way, and you have the right to say anything you want to say. But there are two important issues to point out. First, the tone of your voice and your attitude must communicate respect. Second, once you have said what you have to say, you cannot try to enforce your words through browbeating, negativity, physical withdrawal, sarcasm, or any other measure that he could interpret as disrespect. You will always have the most influence with your husband when he sees you as an ally and as someone who is meeting his mega-need of respect.

If you married a normal woman, she needs security. If you married a normal man, he needs respect. Learning to speak in your spouse's language is essential to successful communication. When both spouses learn to encrypt their language with their mate's mega-need, communication reaches another level as intimacy and passion grow as well.

Allan Kelsey, Strengths Expert

Jimmy has done an amazing job highlighting the mega-needs of men and women in communication. From a natural strengths perspective, there are two communication missteps we tend to take in relationships, whether intentionally or not. We tend to both *minimize* and *project* our strengths onto each other. Unlike Jimmy's message, which encourages us to add security and respect to our language, my message is to discourage us from something: minimizing and projecting. Let's take these communication and behavior tendencies one at a time.

Minimization is any language or behavior that downplays a strength or holds it back from its full potential. Perhaps you feel a little embarrassed about your strength, or perhaps from the time you were little you have been told not to draw attention to yourself and your strength. Sometimes people downplay their strengths because they think they will be perceived as arrogant or prideful, and consequently they back out of a bold contribution because it has been shamed in the past.

It is very common to believe it is boastful to draw attention to yourself. At the heart of this conditioning—which many of us endure as we grow up—is the idea that we are all equally wonderful, so there is no need to make yourself stand out. But as the first few chapters in this book show, each of us is remarkably unique, and to minimize that irreplaceable uniqueness is to rob the world of a contribution that cannot come any other way. We need to avoid minimizing our strengths because of shame or any other reason.

Some people downplay their strengths because of blindness, meaning they simply don't know their strengths are anything special. Our strengths have been with us from our first breaths, and as a result, they feel completely normal. To say they are special just seems silly. As a result, anytime anyone praises us for excellence or remarks at our strength, we just knock it down because it doesn't even ring true. We might think, *Yes, it's true I can do that, but it's nothing special. Anyone can do that.*

This is not correct. Your contribution is completely unique. Although others could replicate a task, no one can replicate your version, speed, accuracy, technique, and insight.

The remedy here is to recognize and acknowledge that you have amazing strengths, and that your unique use of them (as improved by skill, experience, and knowledge) could very well be a world-class performance.

There is no room to minimize the unique strengths you possess. Yes, it's true—we should not boast or be prideful concerning the edge that our strengths give us, but there is no need to hide that powerful contribution from the world in response. Instead, boldly claim the strength you have in your area, and respectfully invite those around you (your spouse included) to do the same with their own strengths.

The next mistake we tend to make is to *project* our strengths onto each other. Here's what I mean. I have the Clifton StrengthsFinder® strength of Achiever®. What that means is, I love to get stuff done. I am a doer, and doing comes very naturally to me.

One summer, I left the house in the morning to go to work, and my two teenage daughters were awake before I left. It was a miracle. Before I left I asked them to do two things: "Please remember to walk the dog and take the trash to the curb, because it's trash day and the guys will be coming to collect it." I have read the good parenting books that suggest you ask the kids to repeat to you what you have said, to help them understand what is expected. So I asked them to repeat my instructions, and reluctantly but accurately they rattled off my request. I left, confident that all would be well when I returned later that day. The day went by as a normal day would, and on my ride home I wondered if I would see the trash can at the end of the driveway when I turned the corner to my house.

As I turned the corner, it quickly became apparent to me that I must have spoken Flemish to my kids that morning because I saw *no* trash can in the driveway. Against my better judgment I harbored the hope that perhaps it had already been done, and my daughters had put the trash can back in the garage. Only a trip inside would reveal the truth.

I stepped inside and was greeted immediately by our dog. He was standing in front of the door with longing eyes, and legs pretzelled together to prevent any accidental leakage while doing "the dance." Clearly he had not seen a blade of grass all day. I let him out, then went to find the girls to chew them out about irresponsibility, how small both the chores were, how they would have taken only ten minutes . . . and so forth. You know the drill.

There is a part of my response to them that is normal parenting. I just want to teach the girls healthy responsibility. But then there is the extra part, where I go on and on about how easy it is to do a simple task. I can't understand why they are not as motivated as I would be to get a simple task done. It makes total sense to me as an Achiever®. Unfortunately, I am projecting my achieving nature onto them and expecting that they will be as interested in getting things done as I am. That part, that projecting part, is all wrong.

The girls have their own Clifton StrengthsFinder® results and their own ways of seeing the world. They don't see it through my Achiever® lens. They see it through their own lenses. When

I'm yelling at them with my Achiever® language, they just look at me as though I'm crazy, as though I'm speaking a different language. It makes sense to me, but it doesn't make sense to them.

This projection thing is really bad. We do it to our spouses, our kids, our coworkers, and our friends. I think the worst part about projection is how condescending it is to those forced to listen to us.

It's condescending because the hearer thinks: *You want me to act like you, using your strengths, when I have my own strengths that are different from yours and will probably serve me better. But you think I will do it better if I do it your way, using your strengths.*

This kind of thinking leaves no room for the reality that each of us has his or her own strengths. We see the world through those strengths because they have been with us since birth. They feel completely normal to us and color the world we see. For me to be effective in your area using *your* strengths is biologically impossible.

Be aware of the tendency we all have of projecting our strengths onto each other—especially your spouse. Instead, learn your spouse's strengths and change your language to include your spouse's strengths in how you communicate. For example, if she has Relator® in her top five, speak transparently about anything you discuss and look directly into her eyes when you speak. If he has Futuristic®, for example, in his top five, include ideas about tomorrow in your conversation and ask him what he is dreaming about.

Also, hold each other in high enough esteem to watch for projection and minimization in each other. When you see it, call it out gracefully. Not in a shaming way, but in a way that says: *I've got your back, I believe in you, and I don't want you to get stuck minimizing your strong contribution or playing it down when it is really quite remarkable.* Help each other see when you might be projecting your strengths onto each other, and find a way to

> BY INCLUDING LANGUAGE THAT RELATES TO YOUR SPOUSE'S STRENGTHS, YOU WILL DEEPEN THE ACCURACY OF YOUR COMMUNICATION AND CAPTURE EACH OTHER'S ATTENTION FAR MORE QUICKLY.

communicate that to each other in a respectful way. Stephanie and I do this, and we have an agreement that we are doing it for our own growth. It feels supportive and loving, not attacking or vindictive.

Strengths Based Marriage Challenge

1. Do you minimize your strengths? Can you see it when it happens? Ask your spouse to explain where you minimize your strengths.
2. Do you project your strengths onto others? Your spouse will know, so ask your spouse. What does that look like?
3. Consider giving each other permission to point out minimizing and projecting in each other.
4. If you have been hurt by your spouse and his or her projection or minimization, take this opportunity to say so. Work patiently toward understanding.

NINE

SPEAKING LOVE IN YOUR SPOUSE'S LANGUAGE

Jimmy Evans, Marriage Expert

In the previous chapter we talked about the mega-needs of men and women and how they influence communication. In this chapter we will expand on this to include all four major needs of husbands and wives. Learning to understand and meet your spouse's needs is the key to success and happiness in marriage.

When Karen and I first married, I thought she was the most beautiful woman in the world. But I also thought she was the weirdest woman in the world. The reason she was weird was because she was so different from me. What made matters worse was she thought the same about me. So we spent the first several years of our marriage trying to change each other.

Most couples do the same. In rejecting each other's differences, we end up spending the energy we have to love each other trying to change each other. And believe me, it is wasted energy.

The only way to succeed in marriage is to understand and accept each other's differences.

Before going into the four needs of men and women I want to make a very important point about meeting your spouse's needs. To succeed in marriage you have to meet needs you don't have. This requires a servant's heart. The best marriages are two servants in love. The worst marriages are two selfish people in love.

Thousands of times in marriage your spouse will have a need that you don't have. If you are only willing to meet a need in your spouse that you share, you are effectively rejecting the differences in your spouse and holding your marriage hostage to your desires. But understanding your spouse's different needs is only the first step. It makes a difference only if you have a servant's spirit and are willing to meet your spouse's needs with a good attitude even though you don't necessarily share the same need at the same time.

Some people have the mistaken notion that in some marriages, both the husband and wife share all the same needs at the same time. They operate under the misconception that if they marry their "soul mates," then they don't really have to work at the relationship. Everything moves effortlessly as they share their lives together in a constant flow of matching needs and easy passion.

If you believe any of that nonsense, then consider that bubble popped. A real marriage requires work and meeting needs in your spouse that you don't have. Passion and intimacy flow out of the shared experience of sacrificially serving each other through good times and bad.

THE FOUR MAJOR NEEDS OF WOMEN

SECURITY

A woman needs to know that she will be cared for by a sacrificial, sensitive husband who is connected to her emotionally. A man meets this need by putting his wife first and by demonstrating that his wife is his top priority. By faithfully serving her and meeting her needs in good times and bad, a husband meets his wife's need for security.

OPEN AND HONEST COMMUNICATION

A woman wants her husband to open his heart and talk to her in a patient and complete manner. This builds a bridge between them and connects her heart to his. A woman doesn't just want headlines; she wants complete information. A husband meets his wife's need for communication by talking to her patiently without any distractions. Set a time and place daily where you have plenty of time to talk. Men need to understand that their wives are much more sexually responsive when they receive patient, loving communication during the day.

SOFT, NONSEXUAL TOUCHING AND AFFECTION

Women want to be touched and held in a soft, nonsexual manner. This makes them feel connected and valued. If a husband touches his wife only in a sexual manner, she feels devalued and like a sex object. A man meets this need in his wife by taking opportunities throughout the day to hold his wife's hand softly, give her a hug, embrace her, put his arms around her, cuddle in bed, and so forth. Again, men need to understand that the more affectionate they are with their wives in a soft and nonsexual manner, the more sexually responsive women become.

LEADERSHIP

Women want to be treated as equals—but they want their husbands to be loving initiators of their homes' well-being. Four important areas where women want their husbands to lead are: children, finances, spirituality, and romance. A husband meets this need in his wife by taking responsibility for discussions with her about these and other issues in the home to find solutions to any issues. He leads in the area of romance by planning special times together without having to be prompted by her.

THE FOUR MAJOR NEEDS OF MEN

HONOR

Men need to feel valued and respected. It is their most important need. A wife meets this need by praising her husband regularly and celebrating the things he does right. It is also important to keep a positive perspective when dealing with problems.

SEX

Most men are more sexual than their wives. This is especially true of younger men. Men are also more visual and want to see their wives' naked bodies. Men can turn on and off sexually very quickly, whereas women take more time and effort. A woman meets her husband's sexual needs by accepting and affirming him and not judging or rejecting him. It is also important for women to meet their husbands' sexual needs at times when they don't feel sexual. If a wife is more sexual than her husband, he must do the same for her.

FRIENDSHIP

Men want to be friends with their wives and have fun with them. They don't want to be mothered or demeaned. It is important to a husband that he is more important to his wife than the children or anything else, and he wants her to come into his world and be his friend. When a man is having fun with his wife, his heart opens to her and he feels a very strong emotional connection.

DOMESTIC SUPPORT

Men should do their equal amount of work around the house. But women have the gift of nesting and turning a house into a home. Even if a woman works outside of the home, it is important to a husband that she is domestically centered and uses the necessary energy to create a pleasant home environment.

Understanding and meeting spouses' needs communicates love to them in their language. It is truly the secret to happiness in marriage and to sharing a lifetime of passion and intimacy.

Allan Kelsey, Strengths Expert

I am so excited about sharing this chapter with you. I have been waiting for nine chapters to get this concept to you, and now it's finally here!

After coaching and counseling thousands of people, I can confidently say that I have found a massive, gaping hole in society. It is around *affirmation*. By my estimation, it is holistically missing in the world today. Sure, we encourage one another and say thank you; but clean, accurate affirmation is so rare that when it happens to a person, it virtually creates an addict.

Lets take a deeper look at this problem by understanding the difference between *praise* and *affirmation*.

Praise has everything to do with what you do.

Affirmation has everything to do with who you are.

Clearly these two ideas are not the same and need to be treated differently.

Praise is what we offer someone who does a good job. Let's say we're at a concert somewhere, and the vocalist sings an amazing song. When it's over, what do we do? We clap and yell and whistle. Why? Because we are sending a message to the singer that says: *Well done! Good job! What you just did was awesome, and we want to thank you for it.*

Praise is a direct response to the actions of an individual. It's worth noting that praise doesn't have to be very specific. We praise one another all the time, but we are not very accurate about our praise. If three guys came over to my house to help me move some heavy things around in my home, when they leave it would be very normal for me to say, "Hey, thanks for coming over, guys. I really appreciate your help." This is also praise, but it is very loose—it vaguely falls in the area of the effort they spent. But it still counts.

Praise has an encouraging effect and makes us feel good. It helps to be recognized for what we've done, and gives us a little bit of a high for a few minutes.

Affirmation, on the other hand, has everything to do with who we are.

Because affirmation is about identity, it has certain requirements. In order to affirm me, you actually have to know me. I mean *really* know me. Your attempt to affirm me has to be accurate, true, and right. If it's off by even one degree, then the affirmation attempt simply falls to the ground. It doesn't work or stick if you use inaccurate information. If you really knew me, you would get the affirmation right; but if you don't, then even a close-but-not-spot-on affirmation can result in the reverse of what you were probably hoping for. Instead of feeling affirmed, I feel manipulated and become suspicious of your intentions. Guarded, I perceive you like a politician who is "shaking hands and kissing babies." Imprecise affirmations leave me feeling suspicious of your motives, and I don't know if I can trust you.

> **AFFIRMATION IS NOT ABOUT YOUR ACTION; IT'S ABOUT YOUR IDENTITY.**

In a marriage context, this is huge.

Praise has its place in every marriage because it honors the spouse for effort and recognizes work that is done. It can transfer thankfulness—an important trait in a healthy marriage—and display gratitude, which is another important component. However, its usefulness ends with acknowledging action; it has no power to recognize uniqueness. Praise cannot say to your spouse: *I see you.* On the other hand, affirmation can and will say: *I see you.* There is no way to truly affirm someone without his or her feeling seen and understood.

You might be shocked to find out how often your spouse thinks: *I feel invisible in this house.* Any version of that statement is a call to be truly seen, and praise and thanks will not cut it. Only affirmation can heal that kind of pain. So how do you affirm your spouse? You affirm your spouse by simply using his or her strengths.

My unique Clifton StrengthsFinder® results are not only indicators of what kind of actions I will value or willfully repeat. They are also indicators of who I am. As you know, I have Achiever® at the top of my list. My Achiever® comes out in the way I swing my golf clubs, in the way I do my work in the office, and even in the way Stephanie and I do something fun together. These strengths are not only what I do; they are who I am.

So, if you want to affirm me, then you need to know my strengths and use my strengths language to affirm me. Let's take my wife, Stephanie, as an example.

Stephanie has Relator® in her top five. That means she *highly* values relationships, and she is truly and naturally fantastic at them. It is very easy to have her as a friend because she is so good at friendship. It comes naturally to her because it is a strength of hers. Because Relators® do relationships so well, they have a high standard for relationships, and over the years, they develop acute relational powers in the areas of transparency, authenticity, and body language. If you fake it with a Relator®, they can tell instantly. Recognizing fakeness in you could cause them to move you to a ring of acquaintance, a few steps removed from the intimacy you once might have enjoyed. Also, Relators® need eye-to-eye contact in conversation because that's how they measure transparency. The best way to annoy a Relator® is to mess with your phone while conducting a conversation. It won't end well.

For me to affirm Stephanie, I need to use the Relator® language to offer my thanks and my recognition. That way, she not only feels her work is valuable and recognized but also that *she* is valuable and recognized. In my thanks, then, it is not enough to say: *I appreciate you. Good job for staying up with the girls to talk through their girl stuff at school.* This phrase is a good example of praise. It's healthy, but the joy and positive effect of this kind of thanks is short-lived.

For me to be able to affirm her, I need not only to thank her for her actions but also to recognize *her.* I should say something like: "Thank you for staying up with the girls to talk through their relational stuff last night. I know that your strong Relator® power helps them feel genuinely heard and gives them a mature sounding board to grow against. I don't have that intuition, and our family is stronger because you do. I love you."

Do you see the difference? One statement—that of praise—simply acknowledges action. The second statement acknowledges action, but it recognizes the unique strength in action. The result is a powerful affirmation. You are essentially saying: *I see* you—*not just what you do!*

Your relationship with your spouse will take a revolutionary turn when you begin doing this with each other. In affirmation, you are essentially saying to your spouse: *I see what you do, and I see who you are—and I love both.*

Affirmations are missing in the world today because we don't know each other very well—at least, not well enough to accurately affirm each other. Consequently, we are all walking around feeling unseen. Affirmation is also deeply romantic, but we will deal with that a little later.

Strengths Based Marriage Challenge

1. Take the time to understand your spouse's strengths.
2. Pick one strength at a time and practice using the appropriate language in your recognition and your thanks. This should feel like praise.
3. Now intentionally use your understanding of that strength in your spouse to affirm something you recently saw in them. Recognize not just what they did, but who they were in that moment. This should feel like affirmation.
4. Ask your spouse, "Did that help you feel more seen, more valued?"

TEN

THE FIVE ESSENTIAL ELEMENTS OF COMMUNICATION IN MARRIAGE

Jimmy Evans, Marriage Expert

In the last two chapters we examined the importance of understanding our differences as men and women. I believe this is the single most important issue in equipping us to successfully communicate. In this chapter I want to tell you about five important foundational elements that will help you communicate and resolve conflicts on a regular basis. I call these the five Ts of successful communication.

THE FIVE "T"S

TONE

I have already discussed this in chapter 8, so I won't elaborate much. It just needs to be noted that beyond what we are saying, our attitudes are expressed by the tone in our voices; and our tone either allows our spouses to receive what we say in a positive manner or prevents them from doing so. You can say exactly the same words in a positive or negative tone, and it completely changes what your spouse hears. The first essential element of successful communication in marriage is to keep a loving and positive tone in your voice.

TIME

We fall in love because we patiently communicate with each other. That takes time. But when we get married, begin to have kids, and work demands grow, time is scarce. Often we don't talk as much as we should. When that happens, not only is one of the most important needs of the wife being neglected but we also begin to feel distant, and the goodwill of the relationship begins to fade.

We simply cannot allow that to happen. Communication is essential in every marriage, and it must be prioritized above children, work, hobbies, or anything else. We must set time every day to have face-to-face communication without any distractions. Karen and I did this at night after we put the kids to bed.

We gave our children quality time every evening, but we trained them to respect our need to be alone together. They quickly learned that we loved them but also valued our relationship. Our children are now grown with children of their own, and they do the same with their kids as we did with them. And they both have great kids and strong marriages.

We had a sitting area in our bedroom, and after our kids were in bed, we would fix popcorn and sit and talk as we ate it. This was one of our favorite times of the day, and it was central to keeping our marriage strong through some very busy and stressful times. This was an inviolable part of our marriage.

When our kids got older, we also walked together for an hour and a half many mornings. We would talk for around forty-five minutes and pray for forty-five minutes. It would be hard for me to adequately tell you what an incredible blessing that was to us.

You must take the time to talk to each other in a loving and patient manner every day. Nothing is important enough to keep you from doing it, and your marriage will thrive as you take the time to talk daily. Make it a daily discipline, and don't give it up for anything or anyone.

TRUST

Communication doesn't happen in marriage until we can do it on a heart level. Communication isn't just fact sharing; it is relating and caring for each other. And for that to happen, we must develop the trust that is necessary.

Trust is always earned, and so is mistrust. You earn trust by being a safe place for your spouse to open up and share his or her heart. You lose trust by not being available or by being judgmental and critical. You earn trust by being sensitive and caring. You lose trust by being distracted and uncaring.

You earn trust by taking responsibility for your mistakes and asking for forgiveness. You lose trust by blaming others and being too proud to admit your faults. You earn trust with consistency and faithfulness in meeting your spouse's needs and fidelity to the marriage on every level. You lose trust by being inconsistent or by putting something or someone else before your spouse.

There is a big difference between talking and communicating.

Talking is something we do with our tongues. Communicating is something we do with our hearts. And because of that, it requires trust.

TRUTH

An important element that allows for honesty in marriage is giving your spouse the right to complain without paying a price. I've counseled a lot of couples, and one thing that dysfunctional marriages have in common is they cannot tell the truth without someone going ballistic. As a result, they learn to avoid issues, and the problems boil under the surface until finally something sets them off and everything explodes.

The atmosphere of a good marriage is one of serving and pleasing each other. If I'm doing something that doesn't please my wife, I want to know about it. The opposite is an atmosphere where I don't really care that much about her and don't want to be bothered by her complaints. When I don't allow my spouse the right to complain, that is exactly what comes across.

TEAM

Early in our marriage, Karen and I couldn't talk about money. We had very different views about it, and we both judged and rejected the differences in each other. Because of that, we couldn't bring up the subject without a huge fight. I will talk about this more in the next section.

But then we changed. Rather than rejecting each other's different perspectives on money, for example, we began celebrating them. And we realized that we make better financial decisions together. Our differences make us stronger. We are a great team when we respect each other and solicit each other's input. That's true in every area of marriage.

Successful communication never happens by accident. It happens as we intentionally foster an atmosphere of safety and intimacy by making sure these elements are present:

- Tone
- Time
- Trust
- Truth
- Team

Allan Kelsey, Strengths Expert

The results from the Clifton StrengthsFinder® assessment bring insight into any marriage through the unique identity of the couple, but more than that, the results introduce a strengths language into the marriage. Since communication is accomplished in part by language, knowing each other's strengths can really change the power and accuracy of communication.

Communication is not necessarily accomplished when speaking and hearing occur. Communication is accomplished when ideas and thoughts are successfully shared between two people. The Clifton StrengthsFinder® assessment gives the world a language to best interact with one another. Your spouse's top-five strengths represent some of the best that will ever come from them, and to use their language when talking with them improves the pace and quality of your communication.

In his book *First Things First*, Stephen Covey argues that we should "seek first to understand" before being understood.[1] This approach elevates the listening role, putting an emphasis on fully understanding *before* offering a response. All too often in communication, one spouse pauses while the other is speaking—but only in order to line up what to say next. This is clearly not about the desire to listen, understand, or even communicate, but simply waiting to speak at someone.

Stephanie's words will come to me laced with the language of her strengths. She can't help it, and neither can I when I speak. But if I am aware of that and I interpret her words through her strengths lens, then it helps me understand her better. Then when I respond, my answers are more likely to be appropriate for her. My agenda will not take center stage. In doing this, I am seeking to understand.

> A STRENGTHS APPROACH TO COMMUNICATION WITH MY WIFE WOULD HELP ME FILTER MY LISTENING THROUGH HER STRENGTHS.

For example, Stephanie has Belief® in her top five. That means she has some core ideas and feelings that are absolutely nonnegotiable. If she communicates with me through her Belief® using very strong language that is firm, is loud, and leaves no room for disagreement, I could respond in one of two ways:

First: *She is really mad about this issue and probably mad at me. I don't know what I have done, but I'm pretty sure I'm innocent.*

How dare she be so forceful with me? I think I'm gonna fight back because I did nothing wrong. (A me-centered response.)

Second: *Wow, Steph is really fired up about this idea. This must touch on a core issue related to her Belief®. I wonder—if I ask her about it, will I learn something new about her? I love her passion.* (A seeking-to-understand approach.)

Seeking first to understand—before being understood—is much easier when you have the Clifton StrengthsFinder® language to provide the insight you need to accurately understand your spouse's communication.

Next, seeing or thinking through a strengths lens will not become a habit without effort. More than likely, it will take some intentional thought to adopt and practice the language in your relationships. It's only once you have consciously come to the decision to adopt and include the strengths language that your communication will change.

Start by understanding all five of your spouse's strengths. Get to know what they are and how they work in your spouse's life. Talk about them over coffee and get more comfortable with them. Read any material that Gallup® produced for your spouse's results, and discuss it with your spouse. Then choose one strength at a time and practice listening for it in conversation. You will find your ability to see your spouse through the lens of your spouse's strengths improving, and your understanding of his or her communication will get much better.

Finally, not all communication is verbal. We say a whole lot with our bodies, our eyes, our postures, and our general pace in life. If you see bright eyes, a fresh smile, bold posture, and a swift step in your spouse, it's easy to deduce that things are good on this particular day. You may not know what provoked it, but at the very least, it should spark a conversation between you.

On the other hand, a slumped posture, a slow gait, downcast eyes, and monotone responses indicate that something is not right. If this happens for a day or so before your spouse springs back to normal, that is one thing. But if this kind of behavior becomes a pattern, then I would like to propose that it could be a strengths issue.

Of course there are many reasons why your spouse would display this kind of disconnected and dejected behavior, but one of them may be that your spouse is not feeling seen and is communicating this fact to you through body language.

Nobody can continue in a role, whether at work or at home, and go unseen indefinitely. Eventually the lack of purpose will be so discouraging that the person will want to leave. Believing they have nothing to contribute, they will leave the marriage or the job. Built into all of us is an inherent desire to express our truest selves and to be accepted—better yet, wanted—for the best of who we are. Your strengths represent the area from which some of the best of you will emerge. If they go routinely unseen and unrewarded, discouragement will set in. That discouragement leads to a sense of rejection, and

> YOUR SPOUSE'S STRENGTHS ARE NOT BEING GIVEN A PLACE TO SHINE, AND YOUR SPOUSE IS FEELING OVERLOOKED—AS IF HIS OR HER CONTRIBUTION IS VALUELESS.

rejection provokes feelings of worthlessness. Live with that for a period of time, and any person would eventually display downcast eyes and disinterest in life.

The solution to discouragement is to do something that uses or validates your design, your strengths. For me, if things seem to be going against me in my personal life, my agitation levels increase, and I know the solution is to go out and get something done. That is my remedy because my number-one strength is Achiever®. I feel most right when I am making a positive working contribution. I know that if I can achieve something, when I'm done I will feel a *lot* better. So I go out and wash the car or organize the garage or mow the lawn. When it's done, I can check it off in my mind. My outlook on life gets much better.

From a work perspective, if you are routinely feeling like your strengths are not being used or seen, the best-case scenario is that your supervisor will be open to transparent communication. If so, you can work together to process your needs and create a role that incorporates more of your strengths. If that is not an option, do the best you can on your own to incorporate your strengths into your job. If that is not at all possible, don't be surprised if you feel pressed to look for another role that acknowledges your design a little more. This kind of reaction is not a failure; it is actually more about self-preservation. Your strengths are not only what you do but also who you are.

Communication when using your strengths is cleaner, faster, and more accurate. The more you and your spouse can understand about each other through your strengths, the more effective your communication will be.

Strengths Based Marriage Challenge

1. Are you aware of how you use your strengths to communicate with your spouse? If so, can you give an example?
2. What kind of strengths based communication would you appreciate from your spouse? Be specific.
3. What behavior do you notice in your spouse that "tells" their demeanor? Is their demeanor downcast? If so, could an underused strength be responsible? What area of life is potentially being unseen?
4. Discuss this idea and explore which strengths may be feeling ignored. Then give an example of the kind of language that would to make you feel seen.

ELEVEN

THE LANGUAGE OF ROMANCE

Jimmy Evans, Marriage Expert

Romance is a daily essential for every marriage, and it is as important for men as it is for women. By making those two statements, it's quite possible I just blew away two of the most common misconceptions people have about romance. Most people believe that romance is a seasonal extra that isn't needed every day. They also believe that women need romance more than men. Not true.

Romance is meeting an unspoken need or desire in your spouse. We naturally do this every day when we are dating and pursuing each other. Romance is why we fall in love. We study each other when we date because we want to please each other. And we do loving things pre-emptively because we know it will endear us to our potential mates.

But as time goes on and we are secure in the relationship, we often don't feel the need to do loving things any longer. Or maybe we just pull out the romance when we are in trouble or for special occasions. The longer that goes on, the higher the probability that at some point we will stop altogether. The romantic rust becomes so thick and the bad habits become so entrenched that we simply succumb to an existence in a passionless relationship.

The scenario I have just painted for you is exactly why romance is such a crucial part of our daily lives as married couples. I told you that romance is meeting an unspoken need or desire in your spouse. It doesn't mean your spouse never speaks it; it just means you aren't doing what you should to meet a demand or to satisfy a frustration.

Romance means: *I am studying you. You are on my heart. I think about you when I'm not with you because I want to. I do things for you because you are the object of my affection and the love of my life. You are not a burden to me; you are a delight, and I love to serve you and please you.*

That is the spirit of romance. But when romance fades, the message changes. Lack of romance means: *I'm not studying you. You are not on my heart. I don't think about you when I'm not with you. I don't want to do things for you because that would be a burden.*

Romance is the language of desire. Lack of romance is the language of rejection. There are two reasons we love some-one. First, there is something about them we find admirable or attractive. Second, we like the way someone makes us feel about ourselves. You simply don't fall in love with a person who makes you feel bad about yourself.

Romance is meeting an unspoken need or desire in our spouses daily to let them know they are on our hearts. It com-municates to them that we desire them. It makes them feel good about themselves and endears them to us. Romance keeps the goodwill of the relationship high as it keeps the relational disciplines of the marriage strong.

Let me give you an example of romance. My uncle Charles died years ago, and Aunt Peggy asked me to conduct his funeral. They had a great marriage of forty years and were very happy. I was sad for Peggy that he had passed away. They were best friends and I knew she was heartbroken.

In preparing Charles's eulogy I talked with Aunt Peggy about him. In our conversation she told me something that explained the strength of their marriage. She told me that every day for forty years, before my uncle Charles went to work, he wrote her a new poem and left it on the dining table.

Every day for forty years Uncle Charles took the time and energy to express in a new and creative way to Aunt Peggy how much he loved her. That is one of the most romantic things I have ever heard, and I can tell you that Aunt Peggy was a very happy wife.

One of the most important disciplines in marriage is to be empathetic and sensitive to our spouses and to preemptively meet unspoken needs and desires they have. We do this by studying them and thinking of new ways to express love to them. And as we do this, we are elevating their self-esteem and endearing them to us.

There is a misconception about marriage that it gets worse over time. The old saying "The honeymoon is over!" embodies that false belief. But the opposite is true. When you work at it properly, marriage gets better every year. And there is no need for marriage to ever be dull and boring.

Romance is instinctive in every relationship at the beginning.

It is why we fall so madly in love and have such positive feelings toward each other. But then many times we get lazy and take each other for granted. And as we do, the goodwill fades and problems develop. The romance that was once so alive begins to die.

All of that is unnecessary. The good news is that it is completely reversible. It doesn't matter how bad your marriage is or how long you've been without true romance in your relationship. When one spouse begins to express romantic love daily, it is powerful. When both spouses do so, it is nuclear.

Karen and I were out of love and on the brink of divorce. We had only negative emotions for each other, but our relationship was resurrected by a decision to love each other and to renew our romantic behavior toward each other. For example, we made it a priority to have weekly date nights. We set aside time every day to talk and be together. I helped out around the house more, and Karen even offered to ride with me in the golf cart while I golfed. These expressions of romantic love in each other's language changed everything. We went from being out of love to being more in love than ever before in a very short period of time. Romance is powerful and is essential to communicate desire every day, to meet needs, and to keep the disciplines of the relationship strong. What are the unspoken needs and desires of your spouse? Knowing and meeting them is what romance is all about.

Allan Kelsey, Strengths Expert

Jimmy said earlier in this chapter that romance is meeting an unspoken need or desire in your spouse. If you have not taken the

Clifton StrengthsFinder® assessment, then you and your spouse probably have quite a few core needs and desires that are still undisclosed or not being met. What I mean is, there are critical identity issues that are central to both of you that you will probably never understand if you don't uncover each other's strengths.

That was true for Stephanie and me. We had been married almost ten years before the true value of knowing each other's strengths became a reality to us. During those years, we did the best we could with the marriage-building tools we had at the time, but never did I dream that I could understand her the way I do today. The Clifton StrengthsFinder® tool has given us such insight into each other and such an accurate language to communicate with each other that when I think about our marriage *before* the assessment, I shudder at what might have become of us.

Because of Stephanie's Belief®, I know that she loves to talk about the things she holds dear and does so passionately. Because of her Connectedness®, I know that she loves the challenge of finding the thread that binds seemingly random acts together. Because of her Empathy® and Relator®, I know that she needs to have deep, meaningful conversations about important people-related things. Because of her low Ideation® and Input®, I know that she is not particularly interested in new ideas.

Knowing her strengths helps me know her.

When I know her, I can meet her needs, whether she articulates them or not. For example, because of her Connectedness®, she has a very good "sniffer" for figuring out whodunits. Her movie choices often include a good mystery—a puzzle that needs to be solved. What makes it even more enjoyable for her is that she beats me to figuring out the whodunits, even though I like to think my Strategic® strength ought to win. Unfortunately for me, it often does not.

Knowing your spouse's strengths sets you up to understand him or her in a deeply meaningful way and gives you a leg up on understanding what his or her needs are—whether spoken or not.

Strengths Based Marriage Challenge

SOME WAYS TO BE ROMANTIC USING YOUR STRENGTHS

1. Make a Date Night out of Exploring Your Results

Print out the pages of insight and results that Gallup® sends to you after you take the Clifton StrengthsFinder® assessment. The first five pages are detailed explanations of each of your five strengths. Take those pages for you and your spouse, and as you read, highlight the phrases in each description paragraph that really stand out to you. Most of the paragraph will make sense to you, but some statements will be more meaningful than others; so highlight those.

Then go on a date with your spouse and switch pages with each other. You now have your spouse's results in your hand—and your spouse has yours. Taking turns, name your spouse's strength; and then read the lines he or she highlighted in the paragraph description of the first strength. Then put the paper down and tell your spouse where and how you see him or her living out what is highlighted on the page. Use a recent example. Next it is your spouse's turn to read one of your highlighted strengths to you, and so on. When both of your number-one strengths have been discussed, move on to your number twos. There are many positive effects that come from this exercise.

- It is deeply affirming to your spouse to hear you articulate so accurately how well you know your spouse. By saying so, you are healing an affirmation need in your spouse.
- Your spouse leaves the discussion feeling truly seen.
- You get to hear firsthand from your spouse about his or her strengths, so you learn a lot about your spouse in the process.
- This experience is so romantic that it wouldn't be surprising if the whole evening ended really well for you. (Humorous quip intentionally omitted here.)

2. Sticky Note Affirmations

For a birthday or anniversary, take the time to read up on your spouse's strengths. Using the phrases of explanation in the language of your spouse's strengths, make single-phrase sticky notes with affirming statements that are strengths related. Then post them all over the bedroom or bathroom walls.

3. Plan a Date Around Your Spouse's Strength

Think about your spouse's strengths and consider the course of his or her life over the last month. If it is apparent that a particular strength has had very little visibility lately, make a date that focuses on or specializes in that strength. For example, if your spouse needs some Competition®, plan a go-karting date. If his or her Analytical® appears neglected, offer to play some chess. Go see a feel-good movie with your Positivity® spouse. Or if your spouse is an Activator®, go start a new project together.

The process of knowing and understanding your spouse romantically will never end as long as you are alive. Orienting those actions around your spouse's strengths is a strong way to nurture the romance in your marriage.

TWELVE

THE POWER OF REDEMPTIVE LOVE

Jimmy Evans, Marriage Expert

As I have mentioned, one of the most common complaints I have heard in more than thirty years of counseling is from one spouse who wants to improve the marriage when the other spouse isn't interested. In most cases, it is a wife who desires to work on the marriage but her husband isn't willing.

Most women are more naturally relational than most men. And because of that, 90 percent or more of all the marriage counseling I have done over the years has been initiated by women. Unfortunately many of these women are alone in their desire to improve their marriages.

Usually the marriage has had problems for quite a while. In some cases there have already been some failed attempts at marriage counseling, but now the husband has given up and isn't interested. Sometimes the future of the marriage is in question. One or both spouses are considering separation or divorce.

The question is: Is there anything one spouse can do to

redeem the marriage when it is on the rocks? The resounding answer is *yes*.

In chapter 4 I talked about the power of change and the importance of working on our own issues rather than believing that our spouses are the entire problem. When we change, our marriages change, and it is essential that we take responsibility for our part in the marriages.

In this chapter I will focus on the issue of redemptive love and how to act in a manner toward your spouse that has the greatest chance of changing your spouse and the marriage. To begin, I want to say something that is very important in the process of redemptive love: *the best person does the right thing first!*

When a marriage hits a bad place, there can be a standoff between spouses. Both are hurt and angry, and both believe the other person is the problem. Because both believe the other person is the problem, they feel helpless to do anything until the other person admits his or her faults and changes. That is why in chapter 4 I talked about the importance of focusing first on our own issues and changing what we can change in ourselves. This has to be step one.

But now I want to talk about the issue of redemptive love. The word *redeem* means to regain something that has been lost. In this case, it means to get our marriage back. Redemptive love is demonstrated by a willingness to do the right thing even though that willingness isn't reciprocated.

The strongest example of redemptive love is Jesus. He died for us before we were doing the right thing. Listen to what 1 Peter has to say about His example:

For to this you were called, because Christ also suffered for us, leaving us an example, that you should follow His steps: "Who committed no sin, nor was deceit found in His mouth"; who, when He was reviled, did not revile in return; when He suffered, He did not threaten, but committed Himself to Him who judges righteously; who Himself bore our sins in His own body on the tree, that we, having died to sins, might live for righteousness—by whose stripes you were healed. For you were like sheep going astray, but have now returned to the Shepherd and Overseer of your souls. (1 Peter 2:21–25)

Jesus did the right thing for us and did not respond in kind to those who put Him to death. Rather, He entrusted Himself to God and did the right thing first. As a result, He redeemed us back to God and has left us an example of how to redeem each other.

Let's take a look at the verses in 1 Peter that immediately follow the text we just read:

Wives, likewise, be submissive to your own husbands, that even if some do not obey the word, they, without a word, may be won by the conduct of their wives, when they observe your chaste conduct accompanied by fear. Do not let your adornment be merely outward—arranging the hair, wearing gold, or putting on fine apparel—rather let it be the hidden person of the heart, with the incorruptible beauty of a gentle and quiet spirit, which is very precious in the sight of God. For in this manner, in former times, the holy women who trusted in God also adorned themselves, being submissive to their own husbands, as Sarah obeyed Abraham, calling him lord, whose daughters you are if you do good and are not afraid with any terror. Husbands, likewise, dwell with them with understanding, giving honor to the wife, as to the weaker vessel, and as being heirs together of the grace of life, that your prayers may not be hindered. (1 Peter 3:1–7)

Immediately following the text about how Jesus redeemed us through His remarkable example, Peter applies this truth to marriage as he exhorts both wives and husbands to do the right thing first to redeem each other when things go wrong.

Women are told to be chaste and respectful to their husbands when they are doing wrong and won't change. When it tells women to be submissive, it must be understood that men and women are equals. Submission is an attitude of humility and trust in God. A gentle and quiet spirit isn't a mousy, beaten-down spirit. It is the spirit of a strong woman who trusts in a big God to change her husband. And because she trusts in God, she doesn't have to act unbecomingly.

The promise to women in 1 Peter 3 is powerful. They are told that they can change their husbands without a word as they treat them better than they deserve while trusting in God. That is the essence of redemptive love.

Husbands are exhorted to redeem their wives by living with them in an understanding and honoring manner. This means men accept and respect the differences in their wives and don't put them down or demean them. It also tells men to treat their wives as equals, as fellow heirs of the grace of life. And it tells men if they don't treat their wives properly their prayers will be hindered.

The bottom line is that God takes it personally when we mistreat each other. God loves our spouses and desires to love them through us—even when they aren't doing the right thing. This doesn't mean we should enable abusive or destructive behavior. That behavior requires tough love and occasionally some very serious action. However, this scripture addresses times when we are suffering because of the behavior of our spouses.

What do we do? We redeem them using Jesus' example. Many of the greatest marriages I have ever seen, including my own, were the result of a godly wife or husband who had the courage and faith to do the right thing first and redeem the marriage.

Allan Kelsey, Strengths Expert

In *Working with Presence*, an accomplished MIT professor, Dr. Peter Senge, is interviewed by the renowned scientist Dr. Daniel Goleman concerning matters related to emotions, proximity, and presence.[1] It's a fascinating audiobook for any brain enthusiast, but amid their discussion they describe an experiment that was conducted to identify the influence of presence and proximity. It has remarkable implications for our marriages.

In summary: Two cellists were invited into a large room separated by a soundproof wall. They were given the same sheets of music to play, as well as a metronome to sync their timing despite being in separate rooms and being unable to see each other. Electrodes were attached to their heads to measure brain activity during their playing, and when the time came, they were started at precisely the same moment. Ready? Three . . . two . . . one . . . *go.*

They both played the same piece at exactly the same time, keeping time by the same metronome.

It was expected that the brain activity of the cellists (as measured by the electrodes and seen on the computer screens) would look very similar since they were playing the same piece at the same time in the same place. That was wrong. The cellists' interpretations of the music were different, so their timing was off. Furthermore, the brain activity screens showed very different mapping. There was no synergy or syncing as was expected.

The cellists were removed from the rooms, introduced to each other, and given time to form a common bond over coffee for an hour. Then they were drawn back to the rooms, where the experiment was repeated—only this time, they were told to play with the mind-set of being in sync with each other. Both musicians protested, explaining vigorously how impossible that would be without being in the same room. Yet the experiment went on, and to the amazement of the scientists, the second time the music was played there were different results. There was remarkable similarity in the brain imaging, and the timing of the music came much more into alignment despite their positions in separate rooms.

The experiments were repeated with other variables to secure the data, but in the end, the conclusion was drawn that people display a capacity called *neuron mirroring.* Neuron mirroring essentially means that one person who has "submitted" to another for whatever reason—in this case, a musical commitment—can literally mirror the neuron activity of the other.[2]

Neuron mirroring is present when:

I have adopted an attitude that attunes me to you. Meaning, I want to work with you, I want to be in sync with you, I want our efforts to be unified, and *I have a reasonable proximity to you.* Meaning, I can physically get within a reasonable distance of you.

When these two commitments are in play, neuron mirroring can take place.

It happened with the two cellists after they met for coffee. They got to know each other, found mutual affinity, agreed to try to play in sync even though they could neither see nor hear each other, and then they did it.

Neuron mirroring explains how some things are caught. For example, I can be thinking and feeling a particular way, and when Stephanie is attuned to me, she can pick up what I'm thinking. I don't have to say anything because her brain neurons are mirroring mine.

That's all fine if my thoughts are not aggressive toward her. But if I'm having ugly thoughts toward her, she will pick up on that thinking— again, even if I'm not saying anything. My thoughts can become actively destructive to our marriage, without my putting them into words. Neuron mirroring can have a powerful impact, both positive and negative, on our coworkers and our kids too; but nothing compares to the influence it can have on our spouses.

> WHY IS NEURON MIRRORING IMPORTANT TO OUR MARRIAGES? BECAUSE AS YOU KNOW, SOME THINGS ARE CAUGHT AND OTHER THINGS ARE TAUGHT.

This is a very scientific explanation for how you know something is wrong in the relationship even though very little has been communicated. If I asked you about it, you might say: "I don't know, I just feel it. I can tell."

What does this have to do with redemptive love, and how are our strengths involved?

To start acting in a redemptive manner toward a wayward spouse, you will need a healthy dose of faith. Faith helps you endure the process and move toward an outcome that doesn't seem possible at the moment. To that end, Jesus is your best answer. He is the author and finisher of our faith and the strongest source of it, so go to Him and ask for help.

Next you will need to change your thinking. You don't want to extend any anger toward your spouse through neuron mirroring. For example, each time you catch yourself harboring unsupportive or unhealthy thoughts toward your spouse, replace those thoughts with supportive, loving, or even strengths based thoughts toward them.

After that, you will probably need to change your language. You can speak life into a challenged marriage, but what words do you use? Which words will invite redemption, build a bridge, and invite your spouse back into a healthy relationship with you? Your strengths will help you, but if they are not coincidentally also your spouse's strengths, then your spouse may not be interested in what you are saying. What you need is to find power in *your spouse's* strengths, to talk about what *your spouse* is interested in. Use your spouse's strengths language to draw him or her back, and use your spouse's favorite topic—herself or himself—to invite your spouse back to interaction and conversation. Engaging the other person's strengths is one of the most inviting and real ways for that person to feel seen and heard, and after all, isn't that half the battle in a marriage? To feel seen and heard?

But what if your spouse's top strengths are low on your list? What if your spouse's top-five strengths are not in your top five? If that is the case, then you have no natural power to be effective in those strengths. Except . . . there is neuron mirroring.

Remember my discussion of spousal transference in chapter 7? That phenomenon is connected to neuron mirroring. You are actually a whole lot better at your spouse's strengths than you should be, because neuron mirroring helps you function in their strengths as long as you are regularly attuned to the person and are within a reasonable proximity to him or her.

That means you can borrow some of your spouse's strengths power and actually be effective in those strengths through mirroring. You can use that power to engage them in conversation around their strengths, and in so doing, you can reengage your communication and your relationship. This is a powerful tool, and a wonderful way to move toward redemptive love.

Strengths Based Marriage Challenge

1. Do you ever catch yourself harboring negative thoughts toward your spouse?
2. What do you do with those thoughts? Dismiss them, keep score, add them up?

3. In a safe environment, could you express one of the negative thoughts about your spouse that comes to your mind—to your spouse? Did the thought surprise your spouse, or did he or she already sense it?

4. Pick the strength in your spouse that you feel he or she is most engaged with, and discuss how you can connect with your spouse around it. Doing so will begin to rebuild a road to connection.

SECRETS OF
SUCCESSFUL MARRIAGES

THIRTEEN

THE SECRET OF EVERY GREAT MARRIAGE

Jimmy Evans, Marriage Expert

He was worth several hundred million dollars and was a friend of a friend of mine. His wife had just left him, so our mutual friend asked me if I would be willing to talk with the couple to see if I could help them. I agreed, and we met together the next day.

His wife was furious at him for many reasons. According to her he was a serial liar and she couldn't believe anything he had to say. She had just caught him in several big lies—one of the main reasons she had left him and didn't want to come back. Surprisingly, when she accused him of lying, he quickly admitted to it.

She then went on to complain that they shared nothing in common. She said on most nights she took care of the kids and he gambled online in his office. Again, he agreed. But he justified his behavior as necessary stress relief from his demanding life as a businessman. And then he did what I knew he would do. He started giving her a lecture about how she should be thankful for all he provided for her and the kids.

He reminded her of the four-hundred-thousand-dollar-per-year clothing allowance she never stayed within. He reminded her of their other homes around the world, jets, and so on. And as he continued to blab on about how much "stuff" he provided for the family, I watched her countenance.

The more he talked, the angrier she became. Finally she'd had enough and turned the tables on him. She said, "You can sell all this [expletive] stuff as far as I am concerned. I never asked for it, and it means nothing to the kids and me. I married you because I loved you and wanted to spend my life with you. But I have no life with you and can't believe anything you say. And until you are willing to tell the truth and give me and the kids your heart, this marriage is over."

As soon as she said those words he began to backpedal. Again, he admitted he hadn't been honest and told her that he would change. He also told her that he had been guilty of withdrawing from the relationship and immersing himself in business. In a softer tone he tried to make amends, but then he made another huge mistake. As he was trying to console her he started talking about building them a new house. He said he felt part of their problem was the way their house was designed, and building a new dream home would be important for them.

Even though he thought the promise of a new home would be the dream of any woman, she didn't go for it. In fact, I thought she was going to kill him on the spot. She was furious. She turned to me and said, "He will never get it!" At that she got up and walked out of the room. He then turned to me with a frustrated and perplexed look, and throwing his hands into the air, he asked, "What did I do wrong?" Even though I tried to explain it to him, I couldn't get through to him.

The bad news is this couple ended up divorcing. He never got it. And the reason I tell this story is to illustrate the futility of money and material possessions as they relate to building strong relationships. To some degree, I believe money is even a detriment to relationships. Some of the most miserable couples I know are those with a lot of money.

The problem isn't the money itself. The problem is that their money allows them to be served by others and to live a life of privilege. They become accustomed to others catering to them and doing things for them. To that, some might ask: "What is the problem with that?" Well, I'm glad you asked!

The secret of every great marriage is a servant's spirit. We cannot always meet our own needs. If we could we wouldn't need to get married. As I wrote in chapter 9, the four major needs of men and women are different. This means for our spouses to be fulfilled we have to meet needs in them that we don't have.

The only way that will happen is if we serve them, but it goes beyond simply serving them: We must each have a servant's spirit. Service must be something we embrace and do with happiness and a good attitude. It's not an "I've got to do this for my spouse" kind of thing. It's an "I *get* to do this for my spouse" kind of thing.

As an example, the absolute most important secret to sexual fulfillment in marriage is a servant's spirit. When two people are having sex to please each other they are in heaven. It is a lovefest.

They are both focused on pleasing their partner, and it is easy to accomplish pleasing your partner when you are committed to serving that person.

But when you have one or both spouses who are selfish and don't want to serve, you have big problems. Again, I can't meet my own needs. And most of my major needs are different from my spouse's. The only hope I have of getting my needs met is being married to someone who is committed to serving me. And, of course, I must be committed to doing the same for that person.

The rich man I told you about earlier in this chapter wanted to substitute something for himself so he didn't have to serve his wife. The problem is that things can't fill the place in our hearts that people can. We are designed by God to need love and care from our spouses. Marriage is the most intimate and important of all human relationships.

In marriage we are a team. It requires two. And both people must be willing to invest their hearts and souls in serving each other. My goal as a husband is to meet all Karen's needs and desires. I regularly ask her if she is okay. That is our code language for making sure I am taking care of her and she is happy. Early in our marriage I was a selfish, chauvinistic jerk. I never asked if she was okay because I didn't care. And we were on the brink of divorce.

Today, I love serving Karen and she loves serving me. Money is certainly a blessing, but our love for each other doesn't change based on how much money we have or don't have. Our love isn't about the things we have. Our love is about the commitment we have to love and serve each other every single day. And that is a common characteristic of every great marriage I have ever seen.

A servant's spirit doesn't cost a penny—but it is invaluable in building a strong marriage and family.

Allan Kelsey, Strengths Expert

The story of the wealthy couple who would not serve each other is very sad, and unfortunately quite common, whether the money factor is the same or not. All too often our default position is a selfish one. What I mean is, unless you and I make a firm decision to act generously—to act in a serving way—serving others might not come to us naturally. We can very easily and intuitively live our lives from a posture that serves ourselves first. This is not the spirit of a servant's approach to marriage.

I agree that choosing to be a servant when your emotions don't feel like it is difficult. But there is hope.

First, ask God for help. The Bible says in 2 Corinthians 12:10, "That is why, for Christ's sake, I delight in weaknesses, in insults, in hardships, in persecutions, in difficulties. For when I am weak, then I am strong" (NIV).

This shows that I can be strong even when I have no power for it, because God can give it to me. Serving your spouse, even if you don't find the power in yourself for it, can come to you when you ask God to help. To see it work, all you have to do is ask for His help and then start.

Second, I believe the easiest way to find servanthood is through gratitude. When I feel gratitude for Stephanie, it makes it much easier for me to serve her and to put her needs in a prioritized position in our marriage. There are many elements in our lives where Stephanie and I see life differently. Consequently we approach life differently, and those distinctions can produce opposition, friction, or combativeness. From this position, serving her does not feel like the logical thing to do. Rather, what comes naturally to me is to serve my own needs. So I need help to get to a place where serving her is possible, and the road that gets me there is a strengths road. Let me offer this example.

Steph's upper strengths include Relator®, Includer®, Connectedness®, Individualization®, and Empathy®—all people oriented powers. Deep, meaningful relationships and the conversations that make them happen are oxygen to her. She thrives on them. They provide the endorphin rush she loves. My upper strengths include Achiever®, Strategic®, Focus®, Input®, Intellection®, and Learner®. Do you see the challenge here? I am missing any relational strengths in my upper list. What this means is that the very things that provide oxygen to Stephanie provide no oxygen to me. I can't run with her, not at her pace—because I don't have her power. However, since these types of lengthy and deep conversations in relationship are where she feels most alive, they provide me the opportunity to serve her.

On a good day, when I am serving her well—if we go to an event that engages her relational strengths and feeds her an endorphin rush in the relational way she loves—I will do my best to connect with the other men attending the event and give her time and space to fill up her relational tanks without limit. On the other hand, on the days when my tanks are low and I don't have what it takes to hang with her relational stamina, we will probably arrive at the same location in two cars, and when my resources to be social and charming have run dry, I can quietly slip out without robbing her of the joy and reward she feels from engaging her strengths.

When I see Stephanie through the lens of her strengths, I find my attitude toward her changes. My willingness to serve her gets much stronger because she is exceptional in areas that I am not. Yes, I could respond with defensiveness that protects my position in light of our differences, but when I consider how remarkable her contribution is through her strengths, I realize how grateful I am for her in my life. That gratitude paves the way for me to serve her.

Third . . . well, my third point was good, but Stephanie had a better one, so I'm going with hers. When I asked Stephanie what she does to help her serve me when she doesn't feel like it, she said her strong desire to connect with me can pave the way to a servant's spirit.

Steph's mixture of strengths makes it so that she is a highly relational person who thrives on connecting relationally. So she starts with her strengths, with what comes naturally to her, and moves away from what comes naturally to her and toward servanthood. Her strengths get her started and give her an endorphin reward; then she uses that feel-good position to stretch toward a servant action that may not seem to have a reward at first. This approach begins with personal reward for her and ends with reward for me, because she has found a way to serve me.

> **I FIND AN IRONY IN SERVANTHOOD: SERVING IS INTRINSICALLY WITHOUT REWARD.**

I find an irony in servanthood: serving is intrinsically without reward.

Have you ever noticed that? If

an action solicits a reward, it has moved out of the *servant* category and into a *transactional* category. I give you this, and you give me that in return. This is not serving—not in its true form. Serving in its purest form is simply doing for another because you know they like it. End of story.

The irony of it, for me, is that when I serve and my heart is pure and not transactional—meaning, I expect nothing in return—I often end up feeling good about myself anyway. So I do get a reward. That is fascinating to me.

You love your spouse and married him or her for all the unique reasons that brought you together. Your spouse's unique strengths should now be clearly discernible—even admirable— and appreciating them should provide all the gratitude and wonder you need to serve your spouse. Find them and celebrate them. This is the secret to every great marriage.

Strengths Based Marriage Challenge

1. What path can you take toward servanthood in your marriage? Is it gratitude, connection, or something else?
2. Can you truly serve your spouse without the expectation of reward? Does your spouse agree?
3. Tell your spouse what servant actions you appreciate the most.
4. What strength do you find easiest to serve in your spouse and why?

FOURTEEN

THE SECRET OF EVERY
STRONG MARRIAGE

Jimmy Evans, Marriage Expert

When Allan Kelsey first saw Karen's and my Clifton StrengthsFinder® results side by side, he was surprised. He told me he didn't think he had ever seen a couple more opposite than us. As an example, my number-one strength out of the thirty-four is Achiever®. It is Karen's number thirty-four. Karen's number one is Empathy®. It is my number thirty-four.

And it doesn't stop there. Many of my top strengths are at the bottom of Karen's list and vice versa. Today, we understand this and embrace it. We realize we are a team and we truly celebrate our differences and use them to our advantage. But before we understood our differences, it was another story.

With Achiever® being my top strength, I am wired for speed. I am a type A, get-it-done kind of a person. My top three strengths are Achiever®, Self-Assurance®, and Command®. I love to lead and achieve. I'm always looking for the next hill to charge and someone to recruit to go with me. I love to accomplish things that I feel are significant, and especially things that help people.

Karen's top three strengths are Empathy®, Developer®, and Restorative®. She is all about people. Karen loves to relate and invest herself in family, friends, and others. She is very domestically centered and is content being behind the scenes and surrounded by people to love and care for.

Our marriage is one of a lion and a lamb in love. I am a strong leader with a lot of vision to accomplish, and Karen is a lover with a heart of compassion and care. And we are a great team today. The reason we are is because we play to our strengths and not our weaknesses. We value each other and both understand our roles in the relationship.

But it wasn't always that way. When we first got married, Karen's dream was to have a close and loving family. She wanted to have children and raise them in a home where we were partners. But my dream was to be a professional golfer. I had played golf since I was ten years old, and I was passionate about it.

When we first got married, if I wasn't working I was on the golf course. I was in my early twenties with a four handicap. I thought if I could just trim a few strokes off my game I could go pro. But even though that was my dream, it was Karen's nightmare. When I would come in the house after playing golf, I could see the frustration on her face.

She let me know in no uncertain terms that she resented my playing golf all the time and that she wanted me home with her and the kids. She was using her strengths to try to help me be a better husband and father. But I didn't see it that way. I had turned my strength of achieving toward golf, and it was an obsession.

Through a series of events and because of my obsession with golf, our marriage hit a crisis point. It was only then that I was willing to hang up my golf clubs, lay down my dream of professional golf, and put our marriage and family first. It healed our marriage and I have never regretted it. And since that time I have realized more and more what a treasure I have in my wife.

Karen's relational strengths have kept me from wasting my life in pursuits that might have won some acclaim or made some money, but in the end would have destroyed our marriage and family. Karen has helped me to understand people and empathize with them. She has constantly used her strengths to make sure my relationships with her, our children, and our grandchildren are strong.

And because I value her strengths I invite her influence in my life. She is simply more gifted than I in those areas, and I need her on my team. But I am also gifted. Even though my strengths were misguided earlier in our marriage, they aren't now. I use my strengths in our marriage to solve problems and to accomplish a greater vision.

With God, our marriage, and our family as our top priorities, we have some important things to accomplish in life. In 1993 I felt the Lord was calling us to start a television ministry for marriages. I am visionary and could see in my heart Karen and me talking to couples and helping them in their marriages and family relationships through a television program.

As soon as I told Karen about my vision for us, she immediately said, "That is great, but I'm not going to do it. You do it by yourself and I will support you." I said, "No, Karen. I see you there with me, and this is something I want us to do together." It took every ounce of leadership and persuasive ability I had to get her in the television studio the first time.

I didn't force her to do it, but I strongly encouraged her. And even though she was reluctant at first, she soon learned it was something she was born to do. She is fantastic at it, but she needed to be led and encouraged. She didn't have the self-confidence to do it initially, and she still needs encouragement today. But that is something I'm good at. Self-Assurance® is my second strength.

I use it to encourage her and give her confidence. We are achieving something great together. After more than twenty years of ministry at MarriageToday, our television program is viewed by millions of people around the world every week. We are making a difference and accomplishing what God has called us to do for Him.

Karen and I have a strong marriage and family, and we are achieving God's greater plan. We are able to do this because we are a great team and play to our strengths and not our weaknesses. We know we need each other, and we truly admire each other.

You and your spouse have strengths. The secret of having a strong marriage is to act as a team and each play the position your strengths have equipped you to play. As you both do this and allow your spouse to help you overcome your weaknesses, your marriage becomes very strong and intimate. It is a win-win proposition.

Allan Kelsey, Strengths Expert

I am a swimmer. I have always been a swimmer. My mom has a picture of me in diapers (*nappies* is what I grew up calling those things), crawling toward the ocean. I have always loved the water. As a result I wound up being pretty good at swimming, and it was a regular part of my growing-up years. At the time I didn't know that God would use it as a part of my destiny, but that story is for another time. When I was sixteen years old I was training with a new swim coach. His name was Dean and he sat cross-legged on the diving board of the outdoor pool where we practiced.

One day Dean pulled me out of the pool, sat me on the diving board next to him, and after an unnervingly long time, said: "Allan, you have the ability to become a world-class swimmer. Your times could be among the top-twenty fastest times in the world. Now, whether or not that actually happens will be entirely up to you." Then he sent me back to rejoin the practice.

That statement blew me away, but I dared to believe him and began working much harder. I went to every swim practice I could, competed at every meet I could, and swam as many events as I could. Sadly my swimming competition times started to get worse and worse. After a couple of months I went to Dean and asked if I was doing something wrong. I wondered if I'd misheard him or if I wasn't trying hard enough. Dean was also perplexed, so he sent me to a physical assessment center for advanced athletes to get a complete physical checkup, to see if something was missing.

I had to show up that early morning with an empty stomach, and they began by taking blood. The rest of the day slipped by. Stretching tests, power tests, breathing tests—I did them all. I got in and out of clothing and swimsuits all day, and by the end of the day was completely exhausted. I was lying faceup in what they called the sample room (because this is where they took all the samples), wearing one of those hospital gowns that are very conservative in the front and super flamboyant in the back. (You know the kind.) The doctor was messing around in the cabinets and putting things away when he asked me to roll over for one more test.

After being poked and prodded all day, I had lost all sense of embarrassment. By this point I was too tired to care what would happen next. I just wanted it to be over. The doctor walked over to me and drove a needle the size of a pencil into my buttock. Right side, to be precise. Then he said, "Okay, I have good news and bad news. The good news is, we are halfway through. The bad news is, I need to remove this, so hold still." He drew that pencil-sized needle out of my muscle, extracting a cross-section plug of my muscle. He then patched me up with a Band-Aid and sent me home. I was not happy, and I limped for a few days.

After about a week, the assessment center called me back for a consultation with the doctors and my coach. First the doctors went over my nutrition and helped me see that I had some vitamin and mineral levels that were low. They prescribed some supplements to help correct that. Then they said that my muscle biopsy had revealed that I had short, fast-twitch muscle fibers that are best suited for sprinting. After discussing it with my coach, I learned that I was best suited for short-distance events. Endurance racing was not what I was made for.

Dean and I changed my training techniques. Instead of doing what everyone did, my workouts were tailored to my muscle type, to suit the nature I had been given, to suit my design. In my new routines the workouts felt easier to me. I wasn't working any harder, but I was working smarter. These workouts took how I was made and amplified it. It was so much better. It just felt right. Pretty soon I was winning my events. I went on to win the South African national title, got a full-ride scholarship to the University of Nebraska for swimming, and even ended up with a world record.

The point I'm trying to make is this: Every one of us is built for something remarkable. We all have truly unique and irreplaceable gifts. Finding those strengths and using them intentionally is like designing your workouts around your abilities. Purposefully amplifying them is the best way to make your strongest contribution to the world—and it is your spouse's too.

My encouragement to you is to become a talent scout. Look for the talent in your spouse and do all you can to amplify it. Don't make your spouse do what everyone else is doing. Use the Clifton StrengthsFinder® assessment (instead of a painful, pencil-sized needle) to determine exactly what design was given to your spouse. You can build your lives around those strengths. They represent some of the best of what and who you can be. Consider adopting the following sentiment in relation to your spouse: "I will not stand idly by and watch while years go by without your emerging into the fullness of who and what you are designed by God to be."

Become a talent scout! Partner with your spouse as your spouse grows into the fullness of his or her ability and calling, because the two of you are one. When your spouse wins, you win.

Purposefully orienting your lives around the best of your contributions will ensure you are living out the secret to a strong marriage together.

Strengths Based Marriage Challenge

1. To become a talent scout, I suggest making a note when you observe a strengths based behavior in your spouse. Note the action, the strength in play, and the joy you see in your spouse. Try to think of a recent example of your spouse's strength in action.
2. Next develop a way to encourage that healthy activity or behavior in your spouse.
3. Work through all top-five strengths in your spouse— noting the action, the strength, and the joy.
4. Boil your observations down to an encouraging phrase and practice, then say it to your spouse at appropriate times. Watch and wait for the response.

FIFTEEN

THE SECRET OF EVERY HAPPY MARRIAGE

Jimmy Evans, Marriage Expert

We have talked throughout this book about the importance of respecting the differences in your spouse. It is crucial to having a happy marriage. In this chapter I want to reveal to you one of *the* most important determinants of whether or not you will experience true happiness and fulfillment in your marriage.

I have conducted marriage seminars all over the world for many years. In my talks I often ask a question that gets the same response wherever I ask it. There are actually two questions I ask. The first is: "How many of you grew up in a home where one parent was clearly dominant over the other parent?" Immediately 70 to 80 percent of the people in the room put their hands up.

Then I ask my second question: "How many of you who just put your hands up believe that it had a negative impact on your parents' marriage and the family?" Every hand that was raised the first time goes back up. It always amazes me that the response is so predictable and immediate.

In most marriages there is a dominant spouse. That means if the marriage is a corporation, then one spouse owns more stock than the other. They have more say in decision-making. Either through force of personality, manipulation, domination, or some other means, one spouse controls the other. It kills the intimacy and goodwill of the relationship, and it is a gender-neutral issue. There are just as many dominant men as women.

Research has proven that one of the most important elements of success in marriage is shared control. When spouses respect each other and make decisions together, intimacy and happiness skyrocket. That is what marriage is all about. When you are sharing control of the marriage and making decisions together, you are sharing life. And that is why we get married.

But when one spouse dominates the other, everything changes. The person being dominated feels disrespected. If it is a man being dominated, he will often feel emasculated and deeply resentful of the way his wife treats him. This often causes him to emotionally withdraw from the relationship, which typically causes more anger and dominant behavior from his wife. The emotional distance she senses will often cause her to become even more aggressive.

If a woman is being dominated, she, too, will feel disrespected. This will naturally cause her to feel insecure and unloved. The fact that her husband doesn't solicit her input and treat her as an equal strikes at the heart of her need for intimacy and connection. The longer she is dominated, the more she loses respect for her husband and any sense of unity with him.

Marriage only works when it is a shared relationship on all levels. When Karen and I got married, I dominated her in every way. Not only do I have a strong personality but also I am a very fast talker. I am never at a loss for words, and I can process information very quickly. Karen is the exact opposite. She processes information slower, and it takes her awhile to decide what she wants to say. Early in our marriage I was a jerk. First of all, I dominated our home and the decision-making. I felt that I was better than Karen and knew more than she did. Second, I didn't take responsibility for my behavior. When Karen would confront me about something I had said or done, I became a "prosecuting attorney" and basically shouted her down and tried to convince her that she was the problem.

We had no intimacy and were on the brink of divorce. But thanks to God and a good wife, I changed. In looking back on my days as a dominant husband, I realize how exhausting it was. It is hard work being god. And that is who I thought I was. I thought somehow I had the God-given right to dominate Karen and our home.

I look back on those years as the worst time in my life and our marriage. Everything I expected in marriage was turned upside down. Everything I expected from Karen was ruined by my selfish and arrogant behavior. Our differences were a mangled mess and the source of untold tension. And much of my dominant behavior was designed to erase our differences and conform Karen into my image.

On the day I changed, I apologized to Karen and asked her to forgive me. I told her I would never again dominate or demean her, and from that day forward we would make all our decisions together. I told her she could be completely honest and I would never make her pay a price for doing so. And since that day, almost forty years ago, we have acted as a team. In our "corporation" we both own equal shares of stock. And in our "corporation" we are very successful and happy partners.

For our strengths to be dynamic and not dangerous, there has to be total equality. There cannot be a shred of dominance by either spouse. In our marriage, we are both submitted to God and we submit the decisions of our home to God in prayer. Therefore, we aren't two stubborn people butting heads. We are two humble and submitted people trying to find the best solution and direction in our marriage.

Dominance in marriage is solved in two ways. First, the dominant person has to sit down and begin to respect his or her spouse and treat that person as an equal. Second, the dominated person must stand up and lovingly demand respect. As the dominant person humbles himself or herself and sits down, and as the dominated person asserts himself or herself and stands up, they will find themselves looking eye to eye as equals. And that will change everything. From that position, marriage becomes fulfilling; and the differences that were once so dangerous become dynamic. From that position—and only from that position—is true and lasting happiness experienced.

Allan Kelsey, Strengths Expert

Jimmy raised some powerful marriage issues regarding shared control, dominance, and equality. Equality in a marriage is so important, but it is easy to be misinterpreted, especially when you look at it through a strengths lens. Because our strengths are different, our differences are often not seen as equal. They are just seen as . . . different. For example, in the unlikely event that two people with the exact same strengths ranking got married, then it seems obvious how the two of them could feel equal. Their strengths would match each other, and their similarity would foster a sense of equality. The situation is more likely to be like my own or Jimmy's, however, where we married women who are our radical opposites. Even if you married someone with two or three of the same strengths as yours, your other strengths color the shared ones so uniquely that they are still quite different from yours.

It's not until you see your spouse's strengths as unique yet equally as powerful as yours that you can mutually submit and live in a shared balance of power. It seems impossible, however, to discuss this idea without it spilling over into the traditional gender roles in a marriage. How strengths relate to traditional gender roles is a frequently asked question, and I want to address it here.

Depending on how traditional your marriage is, each partner has a predictable role. In older tradition, the husband was the breadwinner and the wife the homemaker. If that statement makes you crazy, please know I'm not trying to advocate for or against it; I'm simply identifying some traditional marriage roles. In more modern times, I see a wide variety of balance in marriages where roles are different from tradition. For example, wives are the breadwinners and husbands stay home, or both work. Some couples choose careers and don't have kids. According to the latest US census, the average number of children per family is also declining in America, further indicating that traditional roles in marriage are changing. Even so, expectations around roles in a marriage are a frequent source of argument and disagreement.

It's made worse when one spouse has a traditional role model in mind and the other a more contemporary idea. So how do you settle the issue of equality in marriage and the issue of gender roles?

> **EXPECTATIONS AROUND ROLES IN A MARRIAGE ARE A FREQUENT SOURCE OF ARGUMENT AND DISAGREEMENT.**

The answer could very well be found in your strengths. Let's take Stephanie's and my strengths, for example. She is a very relationally oriented person. She loves human interaction, has little time for mechanical details (relational details are a different story), and is not materialistic. I, on the other hand, am task oriented and love mechanical details, have the patience to figure stuff out, and have an engineering appreciation for mechanical marvels. That's my way of saying I love cars.

For the first twenty years of our lives, Stephanie worked at home raising the girls as a domestic executive (read: homemaker). It was very hard work, and the pay was terrible, but she did it because it was what we agreed would be the best role for her under the circumstances of our marriage. I was out of the house working, and that suited me best. This design was traditional, and it coincidentally matched our mixture of strengths, so we fell into the roles pretty easily. What was not natural for Stephanie, however, was doing the books for our business and paying the bills for our home. She did it faithfully, but it took hours and hours each month and she hated it. It wasn't until about twenty years into our marriage that we switched the bill-paying role over to me. It's really not a problem for me; it only takes a few minutes to complete. This is a much better assignment of roles, and it matches with our strengths.

But what do you do if the roles are reversed and the woman in the house is great with numbers and detail and the man in the house is the relationship genius? Then my answer to you is: Play to your strengths. Let the wife pay the bills, do the taxes, and manage the money, and let the husband focus on the kids, negotiate the teenage relationships, and manage the social calendar.

There are few things more frustrating in a marriage than feeling stuck in a traditional role that ignores your strengths and leaves you feeling misplaced and unequal. It's a recipe for conflict.

On the other hand, dominance can also have a strengths source in both parties, and it, too, is no fun. If one spouse is dominant in a relationship, it is quite possible that the dominance is a result of an overused strength. The strength is turned up so loud in the spouse that its volume simply intimidates the other spouse into compliance. In this case, the dominator can be unaware that he or she is dominating, simply assuming all people act this way. Or that spouse can dominate on purpose because he or she likes the control and doesn't plan on giving it up. Not all domination is loud or assertive. Passive-aggressive behavior or silent manipulation can be just as domineering.

If someone you love is dominating a relationship, try to find a safe moment to tell that person he or she is domineering. Show that person when it happens and help the person understand how destructive it is. Make it safe for the person to see the pain he or she is causing, because self-awareness is the beginning of growth in this area.

The other effect that dominance or chronic inequality has in a marriage is an overused strength on the part of the dominated. If I regularly tell Stephanie that she is less than me because she cannot or will not achieve as I do (which is essentially my projecting my number-one strength onto her), then she will eventually feel so minimized by me that she will feel invisible.

Feeling invisible or unseen is very demoralizing. Eventually, as a method of self-preservation, she will likely choose a strength and keep turning its volume up and up and up until I notice her.

This overused strength is now essentially yelling at the dominator, and the clash escalates and seldom ends well. Instead, I suggest you ask each other if you feel dominated or intimidated. Find out if a strength is being overused, and ask for advice on how to turn down the volume.

The secret to a happy marriage is to contribute out of roles that engage your strengths, to lend equality in decision-making, and to equally submit to each other in deference and love.

Strengths Based Marriage Challenge

1. Together with your spouse, discuss the roles you each play in the marriage. Are they traditional, modern, strengths based, or something different?
2. How did you come to the roles you currently have?

     Were they chosen on purpose, or did you just
     somehow find yourselves in them?

3. If you would like to change your roles to align a little better with who you are, what do you propose?

4. Do you find your spouse to be a little too dominant in an area? If so, talk about how you experience that dominance and explore what may be provoking that behavior.

5. While you are at it, discuss any other marital expectations you are aware of. Putting expectations out there for discussion could help to dissolve some friction you may both have felt but not known how to describe.

SIXTEEN

THE SECRET OF EVERY
DREAM MARRIAGE

Jimmy Evans, Marriage Expert

Shortly after we married, one of the issues that Karen and I learned we couldn't talk about was money. We fought more about money than just about any other issue. In fact, we fought so much about it that it became a forbidden topic of discussion.

But that didn't mean the problem went away. It continued to fester and became a wedge between us. Even after the crisis in our marriage, when our marriage began to improve, money was still a source of great tension.

Karen and I saw money differently, and neither of us could persuade the other to change. But then one day I read a report by Dr. Kenneth Doyle, a financial psychologist with the University of Minnesota. Dr. Doyle believes people see money in one of four ways. He calls these the four money languages.

THE FOUR MONEY LANGUAGES

DRIVERS

Drivers show love by displaying what money has done for them to improve their lives. A weakness for Drivers is that they can be overly dependent on money for significance, and they may be a little (or a lot) materialistic.

ANALYTICS

Analytics see money as a way to ward off problems. Their finances are usually well structured. They are good long-range financial planners. They show love by saving money and looking out for the future well-being of those they love. A weakness for Analytics is they can become too focused on money and things and insensitive to the needs and feelings of others.

AMIABLES

For Amiables, relationships and people are the focus of their financial desires. To them, sharing their money is the way they show love to family and friends. If they don't have money to share, they feel limited in their ability to show love. A weakness for Amiables is they can be financially unstructured and undisciplined.

EXPRESSIVES

Money is acceptance to an Expressive. It purchases respect and admiration from other people, and it is the basis of relationships with desirable people. Shopping, buying, and spending are the ways they gain acceptance from those people. If there is a weakness in Expressives, it's that they spend to hide feelings of pain, insecurity, or incompetence. They may over-rely on money to solve problems and calm fears.[1]

I am an Amiable and Karen is an Analytic. When we fought about money early in our marriage, I called her a tightwad and she called me a spendthrift. I told Karen she was going to be one of those people who died one day with no friends and all her money in the mattress. Karen replied that at least she would have a mattress.

And that is why we couldn't talk about money. That is, until we understood the four money languages. A lightbulb came on for us when we understood that our differences were legitimate and neither of us possessed the singular right perspective concerning money. In fact, we realized that we make better financial decisions together.

When Karen and I were finally able to talk about money without rejecting and accusing each other, it was a huge blessing. Karen told me that as long as we had enough savings in the bank, she didn't mind spending money on some of the things I wanted. For her saving money and being well-planned financially is essential, and I respect that and want the same thing. But for me as an Amiable, I want our family to be together, loving each other and having fun. I want to have a really good family vacation every year where we all get together and go someplace special. And I am willing to sacrifice other things to do it.

Again, Karen wants the same thing—as long as we are saving money and have a long-term plan. And today, we save money and are well-planned financially. Karen's dream has come true and she feels financially secure. And my dream has also come true. We spend money on our family and do things together regularly. And we also have a great summer vacation just about every year. I am in heaven!

My first point in this chapter is that you must learn to respect your spouse's differences and not to judge or reject them. My second goal is to point out your need for each other. Karen and I are incomplete without each other. Karen's Analytic needs an Amiable as a partner, and my Amiable needs an Analytic. This book is about learning your strengths and how to function as a team. Money languages are another powerful example of how this works when you respect each other and work together.

Most importantly, I want to encourage you to be your spouse's dream maker. Early in our marriage I was Karen's dream breaker. My obsession with work and golf broke her heart and dashed her hopes of having a loving, secure marriage and family. Also, I didn't respect her need for saving money and being well-planned financially. Because I didn't share her perspective, I did things that prevented us from being able to save and plan properly.

But then one day I changed and decided to be Karen's dream maker. I don't want to just meet her needs. I want to meet her needs and desires and let her experience her dreams. And today, after forty years of marriage, that is where we are. We are partners. We are a team. And we are in a win-win relationship where we both respect each other and take responsibility for our common dream.

Your spouse is different from you and probably doesn't have your money language. But that doesn't mean there is something wrong with your spouse or with you. You are a team. You both have important strengths and perspectives. Join your strengths together and dream. Have a common dream but also respect each other's individual dreams. As you work together to make your dreams come true, you will find your marriage rising to another level.

Allan Kelsey, Strengths Expert

It really does amaze me sometimes how many daily occurrences of life are influenced by our strengths. For example, take my trip to the bookstore with Stephanie one weekend.

As I strolled around the store reading book titles and wondering what would grab my attention, I found myself drawn to a title: *First Things First* by Stephen Covey. As I flipped through the book, reading excerpts as I went, I evaluated whether or not the content appealed to me. I read the phrase "to begin with the end in mind," and in that instant I decided, *I must read this book.*

What's really going on here from a strengths perspective is that I have the strength of Strategic®. People with the Strategic® strength do *exactly* what that book just recommended; we naturally begin with the end in mind. That phrase made complete sense to me, and I thought to myself, *Man! This guy is a genius. I can't wait to read his book.* I walked off to pay for the book.

On my way to the checkout counter, Stephanie found me and asked me what book I had selected. I stopped, showed her, read her the line that sold me, and then gave her the look that says, "Right? Isn't that genius? You know you want to read this book too!" She yawned and pushed on, unmoved by my compelling pitch.

Well, my first thought was, *Something must be wrong with her today. She must be off her game, because anyone with a lick of curiosity would see that this book is just loaded with gems waiting to be discovered.* A few minutes later she came walking toward me stridently, as if to pronounce the *real* find in the bookstore. She met me in the queue and revealed her selection. The book was titled *Women at War: Declaring a Cease-Fire on Toxic Female Relationships* by Jan Greenwood. I asked her why she chose the book, and she said, "Because it's about relationships with women."

At this point, Stephanie's Relator®, Empathy®, and Individualization® strengths were all producing an adrenaline shot from the title alone, and she couldn't wait to get into the book. In return I yawned and we stood quietly in line, paging through our gems as we waited to pay.

What I am trying to point out is that our strengths act like lenses, coloring the various activities of our lives and making us choose one thing over another . . . and we didn't know why until now. Strengths influence the movies I like, the books I choose to read, the friendships I value, the type of car I like to drive, and the way I approach money.

My Strategic® approach to life helps me forecast what our future could be, based on where we are today. It causes me to get anxious about the nearing eventuality of wedding bills, prom dresses, braces, and the big kahuna—*college*. Not to even mention that elusive and fading concept of retirement! Over the last few years I think Stephanie would say I have become a tightwad, trying to save as much as we can in anticipation of these looming expenses.

Stephanie, on the other hand, has the majestic strengths combination of Belief® and Connectedness®, and this pairing gives her a nuclear capacity for faith. She has a quiet confidence that it will all work out and a robust faith that God will take care of all our needs. She is much less prone to the occasional freak-out sessions that have me concerned about our future.

This way of seeing our future affects our lives today, and it means that we approach the idea of saving or spending money very differently.

Until I knew that her approach was a reflection of her strengths in a way that feels natural to her, I just thought she was irresponsible. I was frustrated that she couldn't see the pending problem we obviously faced. (In reality I was just projecting my Strategic® strength onto her.) I thought if I could just better explain it to her, then she would get it. So we had lengthy discussions about money and spending and saving. But in the end, she just said, "Darling, I love you, but I just don't see it the way you do."

To her credit, she knew this was a point of concern for me and that I didn't have the kind of faith that allowed her to sleep so well at night. She said, "Let's make a plan that helps you feel better about today and tomorrow, and we will work it out."

What a relief that was to me.

It showed me that she loves me. It showed me that she cares, not only about our future but also about the journey of getting there. It solved a big point of anxiety in my life and in our marriage.

Strengths Based Marriage Challenge

1. How do your strengths cause you to approach money? Do you save, spend, both, or neither? Take one

strength at a time and tell your spouse how you see it influencing your approach to money.

2. How does your spouse approach money, and what are your spouse's strengths in relation to this topic?

3. If you allowed your respective strengths to influence how you approached the spending and saving of money, what would the new plan look like? If you like the idea, set aside some time to develop this new plan.

4. Does this conversation influence the roles you play in your marriage? In light of this conversation about money, do those roles need to be revisited?

SEVENTEEN

THE SECRET OF EVERY PASSIONATE MARRIAGE

Jimmy Evans, Marriage Expert

As a marriage counselor I can't count the number of times I've heard a disgruntled husbands or wives utter the words, "I just don't love her [him] anymore." And as they say those words, it is as if they are waving a white flag in surrender. To them, it is the final nail in the coffin of their once passionate and beautiful—but now dead—marriages.

I'm going to let you into the mind of an old, beat-up, but very experienced marriage counselor. And I'm going to tell you what I think when someone says to me, "I just don't love him anymore." What immediately goes through my mind is, *Who cares?* And that doesn't mean I don't care about the person or her situation. It means that person's lack of passion in the relationship is a temporary symptom of a problem that can be quickly remedied.

When someone tells me they are out of love, I can completely relate to it. Karen and I were totally out of love and out of *like*! We had fought so much we were numb and had only negative feelings for each other. At the low point in our marriage, we both believed we had made a mistake and had married the wrong person.

A few weeks later, we were passionately in love, and we have been so ever since. We know what it is like to be on the brink of divorce. But we also know how we got there—and how we got out of it; and we experienced the restoration of the passion and intimacy of our marriage. Truthfully, what we experienced afterward was a much greater passion and intimacy than we had ever experienced before.

Every couple can experience passion in their relationship for the rest of their lives. It isn't for a lucky few. It isn't for those who marry their perfect "soul mates." It is for every couple that is willing to do what I'm about to explain. Here is what Jesus said in Matthew 6:19–21: "Do not lay up for yourselves treasures on earth, where moth and rust destroy and where thieves break in and steal; but lay up for yourselves treasures in heaven, where neither moth nor rust destroys and where thieves do not break in and steal. For where your treasure is, there your heart will be also."

Jesus' words contain the absolute secret of passion in any relationship. He was telling His disciples to invest their lives in the things of God and not to focus on the things of this world. And He concluded with a powerful sentence: *For where your treasure is, there your heart will be also.*

To understand the importance of that statement, let me help you understand the meaning of two words Jesus used in the original language. In the Greek language that the New

Testament was written in, the word for *treasure* is *thesauros*. It means treasure or wealth. But it also means a treasury, or the place where we deposit our wealth.

The second important word in Jesus' statement is *heart*. It is the Greek word *kardia*. It means the seat of our emotions and passions. Here is a paraphrase of Jesus' statement in Matthew 6:21: *Wherever you are depositing the treasures of your life, your passion will be there also.*

Jesus knew if His disciples were investing their lives in worldly things they would lose their focus and passion for Him. So He wisely exhorted them to lay up their treasures in heaven. He did this because He knew an important truth: You cannot separate your treasures from your passions. In other words, you will always be most passionate about the people, pursuits, and places where you are investing the best of your life. Your passions will always follow the investments of your time, energy, and strengths.

Here is another way to say it: Your passions are telling on you. If you aren't passionate about your marriage, what are you passionate about? Car racing, golf, children, work, church, friends, QVC? I was out of love with Karen but passionate about golf. And the reason I was passionate about golf was because it was where I was investing the best of my time, energy, and strengths.

Understanding passion is very simple. Your passions will always follow your investments of your time, energy, and strengths. The most common mistake husbands make is to turn their primary energies away from their wives and direct them toward children, work, or other interests. The most common mistake wives make is to turn their primary energies away from their husbands and turn them toward children, work, or other interests.

But we must understand that when we turn our primary energies away from each other, our passions inevitably will follow, and we will end up emotionally drained or "out of love," as some would say. A spouse in a marriage like that might come to me for counseling. And that person would say something like this to me: "Jimmy, I just don't love my spouse anymore." And you know what I'm thinking? *You're a fast learner.*

You get the passion back into your marriage by reversing the process that got you there. In turning our primary energies away from our spouses and toward something or someone else, we make a big mistake. The result is a lack of passion. But once we begin to invest our best back into our marriages, the passion will return.

This is what happened to Karen and me. We were out of love. But out of our wills we made a commitment to give our best back into our marriage—regardless of how we felt. And after a few days of doing this, we were friends again. After a few weeks of it, we were deeply in love and felt a greater passion for each other than ever before. And we have stayed in love for more than forty years by working at our marriage and investing our treasures in each other. Jesus' words are true, and they are true for everyone.

Even if your spouse isn't willing to invest in your marriage at the same level you are, your investment will change your marriage for the better and can redeem your spouse. Passion is contagious and very powerful.

And remember, the best person does the right thing first.

Where are you investing the best of your time, energy, and strengths?

The first answer should be God. The second should be your marriage. The third should be children and family. And if that is the case, it means your passions are all in the right places and you are headed for success in life, love, and eternity. God bless you!

Allan Kelsey, Strengths Expert

Jimmy has dealt so graciously with the topic of passion and love, and while we are on the topic of passion in marriage I want to explore any potential correlations between sex and our strengths. Yes, I said it. Could there possibly be any connection between sex and your strengths? I believe there is, and I would like to respectfully shed some light here.

Let's start with the basics for all healthy sexual encounters in marriage. Mutually enjoyable sexual encounters in marriage are built around ideas like servanthood (putting your spouse's needs ahead of your own), fun (a pleasing and sometimes lighthearted attitude when the moments allow), communication (accurately and kindly expressing what is pleasing and what is not. Hint: *during sex is not always the best time to have this conversation*), and finally, healthy differentiation.

By healthy differentiation, I mean that both you and your spouse understand who you are and that you are living out of that identity. It means that your identity is clean, that it is yours and not entangled with your spouse's identity—or anyone else's for that matter. With healthy differentiation you are comfortable in your skin and are unselfishly giving away the best of who you are in a strengths motivated way. This involves understanding yourself and being aware of when you are operating in the various talents, strengths, and gifts that you have.

The opposite of differentiation is enmeshment: a cobbling together of what should be two separate and distinct personalities to the point where one spouse cannot seem to function very well without the other. This is a condition where one spouse defers to the other so much that they lose their distinctiveness. They take on the other's traits, and there is no difference between the two of them. They have lost their healthy differentiation.

When this occurs in a marriage, then the thing about your spouse that you fell in love with at first is now lost. There is no longer uniqueness, only sameness. We are not designed this way. Healthy marriages and sex lives are kept vibrant by maintaining our individual uniqueness.

This is not about the exclusion of your spouse, but about the preservation of the identity God gave you.

I can attest to this truth. Recently my lovely bride of more than twenty-three years played a leading role at a women's conference in front of eight thousand people. She had never done that before, so I had never seen this side of her. When I saw her on the TV screen—poised, refined, and collected—I felt attracted to her in a new way. She was being who God made her to be, not holding anything back. In that moment she was quite removed from me and my world. That didn't drive us apart; instead it served to bring us closer together.

> HEALTHY MARRIAGES AND SEX LIVES ARE KEPT VIBRANT BY MAINTAINING OUR INDIVIDUAL UNIQUENESS.

Your strengths and your spouse's strengths are ways to differentiate yourselves in a healthy way. Even if you share some of the same strengths in your upper list, your unique expressions of those strengths make it so that you still see differently. You may both share the Clifton StrengthsFinder® strength of Belief®, yet your personal expression of Belief® will be different. Please don't assume that because you share the same strength you must then share the same thinking. You are unique, and the other strengths on your list color your view such that your thoughts and motivations will be different from your spouse's. Hold on to that difference. Protect it. A happy marriage does not mean liking all the same things and doing all the same things, thinking the same way or feeling the same way. *Happiness is not sameness in marriage.*

Celebrate your differences. Don't just tolerate them, and definitely don't eliminate them. They drew you together in the first place, and they will help to keep you together in the long run. In addition, this differentiation will provide the platform you both need to remain a sexually vibrant couple.

> **HAPPINESS IS NOT SAMENESS IN MARRIAGE.**

CATEGORIES OF STRENGTHS

There is another way your strengths will influence your time between the sheets that I would like to address. In their book *Strengths Based Leadership*, Tom Rath and Barry Conchie address how teams of people interact with each other through their strengths. They point out that all thirty-four strengths are truly unique but can also be grouped into four distinct categories.[1] Below are the categories and the strengths that compose them. In the small boxes beside the strengths I have placed an S or an A if Stephanie or I have the strength. Now we can see in which categories our strengths are most predominantly found.

EXECUTING		INFLUENCING	
Achiever	A	Activator	
Arranger		Command	
Belief	S	Communication	
Consistency		Competition	
Deliberative		Maximizer	
Discipline		Self-Assurance	
Focus	A	Significance	
Responsibility	S	Woo	
Restorative			

RELATIONSHIP BUILDING		STRATEGIC THINKING	
Adaptability		Analytical	
Connectedness	S	Context	
Developer		Futuristic	
Empathy		Ideation	
Harmony		Input	A
Includer		Intellection	A
Individualization	S	Learner	
Positivity		Strategic	A
Relator	S		

As you can see, three of my strengths are Strategic Thinking strengths, and two of them are Executing Strengths. That means I have a 60/40 split, with a 60 percent emphasis on Strategic Thinking.

Stephanie, on the other hand, has two strengths in Executing and three in Relationship Building, so she also has a 60/40 split with a 60 percent emphasis on Relationship Building. These four generalized categories can help explain how we approach many things in our lives, but they are also present in our sex lives. So let's take a look at the general sexual behavior of each category.

EXECUTING

People with a majority of strengths in this category will probably approach their sex lives with some degree of wanting to "get it done." After all, Executers can only celebrate when the job is done—complete. As Executers they think in terms of goals and accomplishment, so if orgasms are the goal, then they work for accomplishment. The upside of this approach is that both parties likely will feel satisfied. The caution is that bringing goals and objectives into the bedroom can bring stress and performance anxiety into a space that should be safe and welcoming. This time together should be a place where intimacy is explored and celebrated, not mapped with goals and driven for achievement.

INFLUENCING

People with a majority of strengths in the Influencing category bring a lot of confidence to the bedroom. Their approach to sex can often be an inviting one and a spontaneous one. Long-range planning for amorous adventures together is typically not a part of their philosophy. They like to act when the moment is right. For Influencers, the process of courting, wooing, and inviting can be almost as enjoyable as the act of making love itself. Foreplay is important, but it's even more important to this category of folks. It's quite possible there could be discussion during sex and even some playfulness. Don't be surprised if this category likes to have the lights on too.

RELATIONSHIP BUILDING

People with a majority of strengths in the Relationship Building category lead their sexual encounters with relationship. Even the very beginning of sex is signaled by strong relational interaction. If you are married to someone from this group, their way of signaling their openness to sex is by sending you relational signals. If you miss those, you will miss the clue. Deep connection and wide-open transparency are necessary for intimacy here because this group has very refined sniffers for authenticity, and only through transparent authenticity can they feel truly connected. For this group, face-to-face connections are very important, and the need for this may even dictate which positions are acceptable in the act. A high level of vulnerability may be necessary with people from this category because this group needs to know their spouses—intimately.

STRATEGIC THINKING

People with a majority of strengths in the Strategic Thinking category are heavy thinkers. It's probable that much of their "turning on" process happens in their heads. Sexually, they know where they want to go and what they think is the best route for getting there. If you are married to one, you would do well to ask what they believe that process/path is. They have vivid imaginations and can dream up all kinds of ways to have fun. It is likely that variety in positions, time of occurrence, duration of occurrence, and even what gets worn to bed will be factors in lovemaking. As long as the relationship and the marriage bed are safe, this is also the group that may like to experiment with new ideas in the bedroom. Planning is important to these folks, so planning ahead for a sexual rendezvous will provide your Strategic Thinking spouse with hours of anticipative pleasure as he or she moves toward the encounter.

In conclusion, I want to point out that the most powerful aphrodisiac in the world is feeling seen and feeling accepted—just as you are. This is not an endorsement for bad behavior or a support for abuse, but for love and acceptance that acknowledge where you are and believe in your future together. Using your strengths to articulate how you see each other and how you believe in each other is an effective way to be seen and to make the environment of your home safe for the growth and flourishing of your marriage.

God bless you as you use your strengths in all aspects of your married life, toward your greatest contributions in your marriage and to the world!

Strengths Based Marriage Challenge

1. Find your and your spouse's strengths and place them in the four categories in this chapter. Discover what percentage of strengths power you have in each of the four categories.

2. Discuss with your spouse what insights you learned from the brief sex descriptions associated with your categories. Does it make you think of anything else you might like to say or ask?

3. Be open with each other about how you can safely approach the activities that will be more satisfying to you between the sheets.

4. If all this talk about amorous activity is stirring things up in a positive way, put the book down immediately and . . . well, you know.

ACKNOWLEDGMENTS

By many measures I am an average man. I'm greying like the rest of the males in my age group, needing reading glasses more and more, and suffering the general degradation that so typically accompanies my age. If there emerges anything remarkable about my life, it is surely because another has made it possible in some way.

Here, I want to acknowledge those whose "permissions" in my life have somehow transferred to me the courage to attempt something remarkable. To dare to dream bigger dreams and more importantly, to dare to believe that I, yes I, might have something worthwhile to say.

To Jimmy Evans, thank you from the bottom of my heart for embarking on this adventure with me. Without you, the help that I believe rests in this book would never have made it out.

To Stosh Walsh, thank you for the irreplaceable courage you have provoked in my life by asking me the most insightful questions. Please don't ever stop.

To my mom and dad, Garth and Rogan, as my first line of relational encouragement you never stopped believing in me and even at a distance I could feel your support. You guys are awesome and I love you.

To my darling wife, Stephanie, the one from whom I learned almost all of what I understand about relationships, love, and marriage. Your persistent encouragement and faith in me has lured me to be a better man. Your love has won me over time and time again. Thank you my darling. Without you, these pages could be filled with flat, egotistical posturing that is devoid of real human emotion or experience.

Finally, I want to acknowledge what a profoundly empowering man Jimmy Evans is. He graciously gave this acknowledgments section to me to use, so the only reason his list of thanks and acknowledgments is absent from this page is because he forfeited the opportunity as a gift to me. This is the kind of leader Jimmy is, and it's why I know his leadership will have impact for generations to come. Thank you Jimmy. You really walk the talk.

Gratefully,

Allan Kelsey

NOTES

CHAPTER 1: STRENGTHS BACKGROUND

1. Marcus Buckingham and Donald O. Clifton, *Now, Discover your Strengths* (New York: Gallup Press, 2001). Tom Rath, *StrengthsFinder 2.0* (New York: Gallup Press, 2007). Certified Strengths Coaches training seminars are held in Omaha, Nebraska, at Gallup's headquarters, where stories and information are taught to Strengths Coaches.
2. For more information on the Clifton StrengthsFinder® assessment, see Buckingham and Clifton, *Now, Discover Your Strengths*; and Rath, *StrengthsFinder 2.0*.

CHAPTER 2: COUNTERFEITS

1. E. E. Jones and V. A. Harris, "The Attribution of Attitudes," *Journal of Experimental Social Psychology* 3 (1967): 1–24.

CHAPTER 5: PROMISES OF PAIN

1. Stephen Covey, *7 Habits of Highly Effective People* (New York: Simon & Schuster, 2013).

CHAPTER 7: THE HEALING JOURNEY OF MARRIAGE

1. Harville Hendrix and Helen LaKelly Hunt, *Getting the Love You Want: A Guide for Couples* (New York: Holt, 2007).

NOTES

CHAPTER 10: THE FIVE ESSENTIAL ELEMENTS OF COMMUNICATION IN MARRIAGE
1. Stephen Covey, A. Roger Merrill, and Rebecca R. Merrill, *First Things First* (New York: Free Press, 2003), 229.

CHAPTER 12: THE POWER OF REDEMPTIVE LOVE
1. Daniel Goleman and Peter Senge, *Working with Presence* (New York: Macmillan Audio, 2007). Audiobook.
2. Ibid.

CHAPTER 16: THE SECRET OF EVERY DREAM MARRIAGE
1. Kenneth O. Doyle, *The Social Meanings of Money and Property* (Thousand Oaks, CA: Sage, 1999).

CHAPTER 17: THE SECRET OF EVERY PASSIONATE MARRIAGE
1. Tom Rath and Barry Conchie, *Strengths Based Leadership* (New York: Gallup Press, 2008).

ABOUT THE AUTHORS

Jimmy Evans is the founder of and CEO of MarriageToday. The ministry's national television program, *MarriageToday with Jimmy and Karen*, broadcasts daily to more than 110 million households in North America and more than two hundred countries worldwide. Jimmy and his wife, Karen, live in Dallas, Texas.

Allan Kelsey is associate senior pastor at Gateway Church in Dallas/ Fort Worth. The former CEO of a franchise business, Allan is a Gallup® Certified Strengths Coach. At Gateway Church, he oversees adult education and leadership development of the staff and congregation. Originally from South Africa, Allan is married to Stephanie, and they have two daughters.

STRENGTHS BASED MARRIAGE VIDEO SESSIONS

You've read *Strengths Based Marriage* and taken the Clifton StrengthsFinder® assessment. You've begun to learn how your strengths are reflected through your relationship. The journey doesn't end now, it's only just begun.

Experience the *Strengths Based Marriage* video sessions featuring more than two hours of exclusive video content with marriage authority Jimmy Evans, Strengths Coach Allan Kelsey, and the testimonies of other couples who have seen their marriages renewed and reignited.

Through these *Strengths Based Marriage* videos, you'll discover how to apply the life-changing knowledge of your strengths and reach the full potential in your relationship.

In these exclusive video sessions:

- Strengths Coach Allan Kelsey gives an informative and entertaining overview of all thirty-four strengths in the Clifton StrengthsFinder® assessment.
- Jimmy Evans shares his inspiring message about how a couple can end the cycle of hurting each other and actually begin to heal the pain in each other's lives.
- Couples discuss how they've learned to appreciate their vastly different strengths that bring balance, harmony, and fulfillment to their relationships.
- Strengths Coach Allan Kelsey interviews Jimmy and Karen Evans and discusses their Clifton StrengthsFinder® assessment and how they've overcome the heartache of a destructive marriage.

To access these videos and take your *Strengths Based Marriage* experience to another level, visit *Strengths Based Marriage* online.

VIDEO CONTENT ACCESS
strengthsmarriage.com/code
Enter the code: strengths4marriage!